EDWARD ALBEE:
AN ANNOTATED BIBLIOGRAPHY

AMS Studies in Modern Literature. No. 6

ISSN 0270-2983

Other titles in this series:

No. 1. Richard E. Amacher and Margaret F. Rule, compilers. *Edward Albee at Home and Abroad: A Bibliography, 1958 to June 1968.* 1973.
No. 2. Richard Morgan, ed. *Kenneth Patchen: A Collection of Essays.* 1977.
No. 3. Philip Grover, editor. *Ezra Pound, the London Years, 1908–1920.* 1978.
No. 4. Daniel J. Casey and Robert E. Rhodes, eds. *Irish-American Fiction: Essays in Criticism.* 1979.
No. 5. Iska Alter. *The Good Man's Dilemma: Social Criticism in the Fiction of Bernard Malamud.* 1980.

EDWARD ALBEE

An Annotated Bibliography
1968–1977

Charles Lee Green

AMS PRESS, INC.
New York, N.Y.

Library of Congress Cataloging in Publication Data

Green, Charles Lee.
　Edward Albee, an annotated bibliography, 1968–1977.

　(AMS studies in modern literature; no. 6)
　Includes indexes.
　1. Albee, Edward, 1928–　　—Bibliography.
I. Title.　II. Series.
Z8021.17.G73　　016.812′54　　79-8633
ISBN 0-404-18014-0

Copyright © 1980 by AMS Press, Inc.
All rights reserved.

MANUFACTURED IN THE UNITED STATES
OF AMERICA

For Billy and Leroy Green

Preface

The goal of this bibliography has been to supplement and complement the English language section of Richard E. Amacher and Margaret F. Rule's *Edward Albee At Home and Abroad: A Bibliography* (New York: AMS, 1973). Amacher and Rule have extensively covered published works on and by Albee in England and America from 1958 to June 1968. Without duplicating their work, I have made a compilation of published works by Albee since 1945 and annotated published material about Albee from 1958 to December 1977. The bulk of the material in this book, however, falls between 1968 and 1977.

My organization differs from Amacher and Rule's study in several areas: 1) chronological listing of data (with the exception of published works written by Albee); 2) sections for unpublished material pertaining to Albee and its location in United States collections, interviews, and biographical material; 3) an extensive list of Albee's plays in collections; and 4) an appendix containing a list of library resources consulted, contributing authors, and the location of materials on a specific Albee play within the thesis.

The collection is not complete because: 1) reviews of premier productions, out-of-town tryouts, or notable productions, and other newspaper articles outside the principal New York dailies and the London *Times* have been restricted to those readily available in reprints in the libraries utilized; 2) because Albee is mentioned in countless secondary sources, discretion was used to determine which articles and books would best benefit the scholar; and 3) several indices consulted have not compiled reference guides up to December 1977.

I have attempted to abstract objectively the major theses in the articles by or about Albee. Those annotations derived from such reference sources as *Masters Abstracts* are cited. Items not seen have merely been listed, with the exception of annotations of unpublished materials in the Manuscripts and Special Collections section supplied through correspondence with various universities.

The bibliographic form for citations follows *A Manual of Style* (12th ed. rev. Chicago and London: University of Chicago Press, 1969). Journal abbreviations were based on Leland Alkire's *Periodical Title Abbreviations* (2d ed. Detroit: Gale, 1977).

Acknowledgments

I am indebted to the following persons for their assistance: *Glyn O'Malley*, assistant to Edward Albee; *Kenneth A. Lohf*, Librarian for Rare Books and Manuscripts, Columbia University; *Jane A. Combs*, Administrative Assistant, Hoblitzelle Theatre Arts Library, Humanities Research Center, University of Texas at Austin; *Margaret F. Sax*, Assistant Curator, The Watkinson Library, Trinity College; *Charles Niles*, Manuscript Technician, Mugar Memorial Library, Boston University; *Kathy E. Wyss*, Manuscripts Department, Lilly Library, Indiana University; *Carolyn A. Davis*, Manuscripts Librarian, Syracuse University; *Paul Myers*, Curator Theater Collection, Library and Museum of the Performing Arts, New York Public Library at Lincoln Center; *T.A. Kumatz*, Assistant Director, Pratt Institute Library; *Ellen S. Dunlap*, Research Librarian, Humanities Research Center, University of Texas at Austin; *Connecticut*, *Walter A. Forbes*, Publisher; *Kenneth W. Duckett*, Curator Special Collections, Southern Illinois University at Carbondale; *Rosemary L. Cullen*, Special Collections Librarian, Harris Collection, John Hay Library, Brown University; *John Dobson*, Head Special Collections, University of Tennessee; *Hortense Zera*, Librarian, American Academy and Institute of Art and Letters; *Dr. Barry Daniels; Dr. Faye Julian; Dr. Thomas Cooke; Dr. Robert Glenn; Beverly White; Vicki Misenheimer; Jerry Neill; David May; Cindi Parris;* and *Mary Lea Latimer.*

Table of Contents

Preface	vii
Acknowledgments	ix
List of Abbreviations	xiii

Primary Sources

Manuscripts and Special Collections	3
Plays	8
Other Published Works by Albee	12
Interviews	14

Secondary Sources

Biography	23
Criticism	33

Library Resources Consulted

Bibliographies of Bibliographies	127
Book Lists and Records of Publication	128
Newspapers, Magazines, and Miscellaneous Indexes	128

Dissertations, Theses, and Research in Progress 130
Manuscripts and Special Collections in the U.S. 131
Biography 132
Plays in Collections and Periodicals 132
Literature 133
Drama 135

Appendices

A. Contributing Authors Index 139
B. Play Titles Index 145

List of Abbreviations

AM	*America*
A.L.S.	Autographed Letter Signed
AO	*All Over*
AQ	*Arizona Quarterly*
B	*Bartleby*
BM	*Box, and Quotations from Chairman Mao Tse-Tung*
BP	*Best Plays* Series
BS	*The Death of Bessie Smith*
CD	*Comparative Drama*
CEA	*College English Association Critic*
Cim R	*Cimarron Review*
CLA	*College Language Association Journal*
CLM	*Choate Literary Magazine*
Ces	*Costerus*
CSM	*Christian Science Monitor*
CW	*Counting the Ways*
Cwealth	*Commonwealth*
DA	*Dissertation Abstracts (International)*
DB	*A Delicate Balance*
DS	*Drama Survey*
Ex	*Explicator*
EG	*Everything in the Garden*
ETJ	*Educational Theatre Journal*
ForumH	*Forum* (Houston)

FY	*Fam and Yam*
HC	*Hartford Courant* (Conn.)
HR	*Hudson Review*
Hum	*Humanist*
K	*Kaleidograph*
L	*Listening*
L	Letter(s)
LJ	*Library Journal*
LT	(London) *Times*
M	*Malcolm*
MA	*Masters Abstracts*
Mao	*Quotations from Chairman Mao Tse-Tung*
MD	*Modern Drama*
N	*Nation*
NashB	*Nashville Banner* (Tenn.)
NBFTV	*Newsbank (Film and Television)*
NBL	*Newsbank (Literature)*
NBPA	*Newsbank (Performing Arts)*
NCL	*Notes on Contemporary Literature*
NewR	*New Republic*
NO	*National Observer*
NR	*National Review*
NW	*Newsweek*
NY	*New Yorker*
NYDN	*New York Daily News*
NYM	*New York Magazine*
NYP	*New York Post*
NYT	*New York Times*
NYTBE	*New Yorks Times Biographical Editon*
NYTCR	*New York Theater Critics Reviews*
NYTFR	*New York Times Film Reviews, 1958–1968*
OT	*Oakland Tribune* (Calif.)
P	*Players Magazine*

PJ	Providence Journal
PP	Plays and Players
PW	Publishers Weekly
QJS	Quarterly Journal of Speech
QTR	Drama: The Quarterly Theatre Review
RALS	Resources for American Literature Study
Ren	Renascence
S	Serif
SB	The Sandbox
SC	The Ballad of the Sad Cafe
SFE	San Francisco Examiner
SR	Saturday Review
T	Time
TA	Tiny Alice
TLS	Times Literary Supplement
T.L.S.	Typed Letter Signed
VV	*Village Voice*
VW	*Who's Afraid of Virginia Woolf?*
WSJ	*Wall Street Journal*
WWD	*Women's Wear Daily*

Primary Sources

Primary Sources

MANUSCRIPTS AND SPECIAL COLLECTIONS

Connecticut

Trinity College
Watkinson Library
Hartford, CT 06106

1. 2 and 9 Jan. 1966
   One typescript of the Dorothy Gordon Youth Forum "Is the American Theatre in a Vacuum?" Part II. Albee was a guest speaker on the programme which appeared on WNBC-TV and Radio. Panelists were Dianne Young, New York University; Leona Faber, City College, New York; Robert Reilly, Most Holy Trinity High School, Brooklyn; Buddy Davis, Jersey Preparatory School, Paterson.
2. 1966
   One theatre script for the play *Malcolm*.

Illinois

Southern Illinois
University at Carbondale
Morris Library
Carbondale, IL 62901
Black Sun Press Archives

    3. 6 July 1964
       Caresse Crosby to Albee.
    4. 26 Aug. 1964
       Albee to Caresse Crosby.
    5. No date
       Albee to Caresse Crosby.

Indiana

Indiana University
Lilly Library
Bloomington, IN 47401

    6. No date
       One mimeographed copy of "The Ballad of the Sad Cafe" with erratic pagination, some holographic changes, and notes made by one of the performers of the play. 218 pp.

Massachusetts

Boston University
Mugar Memorial Library
771 Commonwealth Ave.
Boston, MS 02215
Roddy McDowall Collection

    7. 18 Oct. 1965
       One typescript by author on Judy Garland (See

McDowall, Roddy. *Double Exposure.* New York: Delacorte, 1966, p. 198.)
8. 18 Oct. 1965
One T.L.S. accompanies the manuscript granting McDowall rights to the typescript on Judy Garland.

New York

American Academy of Arts and Letters
633 W. 155th St.
New York, NY 10032

9. No date
Correspondence dealing mostly with business matters pertaining to the Academy-Institute; citations for the awardees, Lanford Wilson and Sam Shepard; reports on poets, Kenneth Koch and John Ashberry; and newspaper clippings.

Columbia University
Butler Library
New York, NY 10027

10. 1961–63
Three T.L.S. to Leah Salisbury.
11. 6 Nov. 1962
One T.L.S. to Ethel Cohen of the ESCO Fund Committee. Permission required to see.
12. 13 Apr. 1965
One T.L.S. to John Leggett of Harper and Row. 1 p.

Library and Museum of the Performing Arts
New York Public Library
Lincoln Center
111 Amsterdam Ave.
New York, NY 10023

Library and Museum of the Performing Arts *(continued)*

13. 5 Apr. 1960
    One L.S. to Robert Kingery.
14. 23 June 1960
    One L.S. to George Freedley.
15. 17 June and 15 Aug. 1961
    Two L.S. to George Freedley.
16. 8 Dec. 1962
    One L.S. to George Freedley.
17. 30 June 1963
    L. to Frank Q. Ware, re investing *SC*.
18. 19 May and 22 July 1963
    Two L.S. to Cheryl Crawford, re *SC* and regret over missing Board meetings, etc.
19. 20 Aug. 1963
    One L.S. to investors, *VW*.
20. No date
    One Christmas card.
21. No date
    Copies of all plays from the first draft through the completed script; clippings, programmes, reviews, and photographs of Albee's productions.

Syracuse University
George Arents Research Library
Syracuse, NY 13210
Mike Wallace Collection

22. 15 Feb. 1961
    One script of a Mike Wallace/Albee interview. Subjects discussed are Albee's plays, and his reasons for being an angry young man. 7 pp.

Texas

University of Texas
Hoblitzelle Theatre Arts Library
Humanities Research Center
Austin, TX 78712
Julian Beck Collection

>23. 25 Nov. 1962, 14 May and 14 Aug. 1963
Three typed carbon copy letters from Beck to Albee.
>24. 12 May 1964
Affidavit by Albee re Julian and Judith Malina Beck.

William H. Crain Collection

>25. 19 Sept. 1960
One T.L.S. to Bob Livingston concerning Livingston's failure to write. Albee says he is well on his way to a Pulitzer Prize and producers want *BS* and *AD*, etc.
>26. 20 July
One T.L.S. to Harry Joe concerning rehearsals of *ZS*, their comparing of notes about theories of the play, the negative aspects of the New York production, Albee's popularity in Europe, Dick Barr's organization of *AD*, etc.

John Gassner Collection

>27. 8 Dec. 1962
One T.L.S. to Gassner over National Theatre Conference invitation and the inclusion of *VW* in Gassner's theatre anthology.
>28. 8 Dec. 1962
One photostat of a T.L.S. to George Freedley concern-

ing an invitation to the National Theatre Conference.
29. 30 June 1963
One T.L.S. to Gassner complimenting his understanding of the "musical nature" of *VW* in his review of the recording.
30. 13 Aug. 1964
One T.L.S. to Gassner concerning Albee's sending an article for a book.
31. 19 Jan. 1965
A.L.S. to Gassner concerning Gassner's "good show" telegram for the opening night of *Malcolm*.

James Purdy Collection

32. 12 and 19 Dec. 1967
One autographed note and an autographed invitation to Purdy.

Uncatalogued Collections

33. No date
One mimeo script of *BM* and one filmscript of *VW*.

PLAYS

American Editions and Anthologies

34. *All Over.* New York: S. French, 1970 [sic].
35. *All Over.* New York: Atheneum, 1971.
36. *All Over.* New York: Pocket Books, 1974.
37. *The American Dream.* In *Drama: An Introductory Anthology.* Edited by Otto Reinert. Boston: Little, Brown, and Co., 1964.
38. *The American Dream.* In *Literary Types and Themes.*

Edited by Maurice Basil, et al. 2d ed. New York: Rinehart and Winston, 1971.
39. *The Ballad of the Sad Cafe.* New York: Dramatists Play Service, 1963.
40. *The Ballad of the Sad Cafe.* New York: H. Wolff, 1963.
41. *Box* and *Quotations from Chairman Mao Tse-Tung.* New York: Atheneum, 1969.
42. *Box* and *Quotations from Chairman Mao Tse-Tung.* New York: Dramatists Play Service, 1969.
43. *Box* and *Quotations from Chairman Mao Tse-Tung.* New York: Pocket Books, 1970.
44. *Box* and *Quotations from Chairman Mao Tse-Tung.* New York: Studio Duplicating Service, n.d.
45. *Counting the Ways and Listening.* New York: Atheneum, 1977.
46. *A Delicate Balance.* New York: Pocket Books, 1967.
47. *Everything in the Garden.* New York: Russell Reproduction Studio, 1967(?).
48. *Everything in the Garden.* New York: Atheneum, 1968.
49. *Everything in the Garden.* New York: Dramatists Play Service, 1968.
50. *Malcolm.* New York: Dramatists Play Service, 1966.
51. *The Sandbox.* In *Best Short Plays, 1959–60.* Edited by Margaret Mayorga. Boston: Beacon, 1961.
52. *The Sandbox.* In *Modern Drama for Analysis.* Edited by Paul M. Cubeta. 3d ed. New York: Holt, Rinehart, and Winston, 1962.
53. *The Sandbox.* In *The American Experience: Drama.* Edited by Marjorie Wescott Barrows, et al. Rev. ed. New York: Macmillan, 1968.
54. *The Sandbox.* In *Reading Literature: Reading Drama.* Edited by Joseph Henry Satin. Part III. 2d ed. Boston: Houghton Mifflin, 1968.
55. *The Sandbox.* In *Twelve American Plays, 1920–1960.* Edited by Richard Corbin and Miriam Balf. New York: Scribner, 1969.

56. *The Sandbox.* In *Literature: Structure, Sound and Sense.* Compiled by Laurence Perrine. 2d ed. New York: Harcourt, Brace, Jovanovich, 1974.
57. *Schism. Choate Literary Magazine* 20 (May 1946): 87–110.
58. *Seascape.* New York: Atheneum, 1975.
59. *Seascape.* New York: Dramatists Play Service, 1975.
60. *Tiny Alice.* In *America's Lost Plays.* Dodd, Mead, and Co., 1965.
61. *Tiny Alice.* New York: Pocket Books, 1966.
62. *Tiny Alice.* In *Best American Plays,* 6th series, 1963–1967. Edited by John Gassner and Clive Barnes. New York: Crown, 1971.
63. *Who's Afraid of Virginia Woolf?* New York: Dramatists Play Service, 1962.
64. *Who's Afraid of Virginia Woolf?* In *America's Lost Plays.* New York: Dodd, Mead, and Co., 1963.
65. *Who's Afraid of Virginia Woolf?* In *Best American Plays,* 5th series, 1957–1963. Edited by John Gassner. New York: Crown, 1963.
66. *Who's Afraid of Virginia Woolf?* In *Fifty Best Plays of the American Theater.* Volume 4. Edited by John Gassner and Clive Barnes. New York: Crown, 1969.
67. *Who's Afraid of Virginia Woolf?* In *A Treasury of the Theatre.* Edited by John Gassner and Bernard F. Dukore. 4th ed. New York: Simon and Schuster, 1970.
68. *Who's Afraid of Virginia Woolf?* In *Classic Through Modern Drama: An Introductory Anthology.* Edited by Otto Reinert. Boston: Little, Brown, 1970.
69. *The Zoo Story.* In *Famous American Plays of the 1950s.* Edited by Lee Strasberg. New York: Dell, 1962.
70. *The Zoo Story.* In *Modern Drama: Alternate Edition.* Edited by Otto Reinert. 2d ed. Boston: Little, Brown, 1966.
71. *The Zoo Story.* In *Classics of the Modern Theater: Realism and After.* Edited by Alvin B. Kernan. New York: Harcourt, Brace, 1965.

Annotated Bibliography 1968 – 1977

72. *The Zoo Story.* In *Twentieth Century Drama: England, Ireland [and] the United States.* Edited by Ruby Cohn and Bernard F. Dukore. 2d ed. New York: Random House, 1966.
73. *The Zoo Story.* In *The Dramatic Moment.* Edited by Eugene M. Waith. Englewood Cliffs, N.J.: Prentice-Hall, 1967.
74. *The Zoo Story.* In *Contexts of the Drama: The Greeks to Contemporary American Theatre.* Compiled by Richard Goldstone. New York: McGraw-Hill, 1968.
75. *The Zoo Story.* In *Reading for Understanding: Fiction, Drama, Poetry.* Compiled by Caroline Shrodes, et al. New York: Macmillan, 1968.
76. *The Zoo Story.* In *Literature of America.* Volume 2. Compiled by Irving Howe, et al. 2d ed. New York: McGraw Hill, 1971.

English Editions and Anthologies

77. *All Over.* London: Jonathan Cape, 1972.
78. *The American Dream.* In *New American Drama.* Edited by Charles Marowitz. Harmondsworth: Penguin, 1966.
79. *The American Dream: Play.* London: Samuel French, n.d.
80. *Box* and *Quotations from Chairman Mao Tse-Tung.* London: Jonathan Cape, 1970.
81. *Box* and *Quotations from Chairman Mao Tse-Tung.* London: Penguin, 1972.
82. *The Death of Bessie Smith.* London: S. French, 1960.
83. *A Delicate Balance.* Harmondsworth: Penguin, 1969.
84. *Malcolm.* London: Jonathan Cape with Secker and Warburg, 1967.
85. *The Sandbox.* In *Theatre Today.* Edited by David Morgan Thompson. London: Longmans, 1965.
86. *Seascape.* London: Jonathan Cape, 1976.
87. *Tiny Alice, Box,* and *Quotations from Chairman Mao Tse-Tung.* Harmondsworth: Penguin, 1971.

88. *Who's Afraid of Virginia Woolf?* 3d ed. London: Penguin, 1970.
89. *Albee's Who's Afraid of Virginia Woolf?* London: McGraw-Hill, n.d.
90. *The Zoo Story.* In *Absurd Drama.* Edited by Martin Esslin. Harmondsworth: Penguin, 1965.

OTHER PUBLISHED WORKS BY ALBEE

Articles

91. "Chaucer: The Legend of Phyllis." *CLM,* 32 (1945): 59–63.
92. "The Decade of Engagement." *SR,* 24 Jan. 1970, pp. 19–20.

   Albee states that serious theater has emerged and been accepted during the 1960s. An attitude of disengagement which has appeared at the end of the decade, however, must be fought if the arts are to survive.

93. "Here Is a Resume of the Guild's Proposed Off-Broadway Contract." *Dramatists Guild Quarterly,* 8(1973): 33–35.

   The Dramatists Guild has devised a Minimum Basic Contract for Off-Broadway productions "to protect small house dramatists" in the New York City area.

94. "Richard Strauss." *CLM,* 31 (1945): 87–93.
95. "Wants to Know Why." *NYT,* 7 Oct. 1962, sec. 2, p. 1.

   Albee questions the importance of Broadway over Off-Broadway.

Prose

96. "Empty Tea." *CLM*, 31 (May 1945): 43-44.
97. "Lady With an Umbrella." *CLM*, 20 (May 1946): 5-10.
98. "L'Apres-midi d'une faune." *CLM*, 31 (1945): 43-44.
99. "A Place on the Water." *CLM*, 32 (1945): 15-18.
100. "Sort of a Test." *CLM*, 32 (Nov. 1945): 45-47.
101. "Well, It's Like This." *CLM*, 32 (1945): 5-10.

Poetry

102. "Associations." *CLM*, 31 (May 1945): 15-16.
103. "Chopin." *K*, 18 (Sept. 1946): 12. Reprinted in "Two Early Poems by Edward Albee," compiled by Phillip C. Kolin, *RALS*, 5 (1975): 95-97.
104. "Eighteen." *K*, 17 (Sept. 1945): 15. Reprinted in "Two Early Poems by Edward Albee," compiled by Phillip C. Kolin, *RALS*, 5 (1975): 95-97.
105. "Frustration," and "Sonnet." *CLM*, 31 (May 1945): 60.
106. "Interlude." *CLM*, 32 (1946): 29.
107. "Monologue," "The Atheist," and "Sonnet." *CLM*, 20 (1945): 10.
108. "Nihilist." *CLM*, 32 (May 1946): 22. Reprinted in *Albee*, compiled by C.W.E. Bigsby, p. 4. Edinburgh: Oliver and Boyd, 1969.
109. "Old Laughter." *CLM*, 31 (1944): 37-38.
110. "Peaceable Kingdom, France." *NYT*, 29 Dec. 1975, p. 51.
111. "Question." *CLM*, 31 (1945): 81.
112. "Reunion." *CLM*, 32 (1945): 71-72.
113. "To a Gold Chain Philosopher at Luncheon." *CLM*, 31 (1945): 34.
114. "To a Maniac." *CLM*, 20 (May 1946): 71. Reprinted in *Albee*, compiled by C.W.E. Bigsby, pp. 3-4. Edinburgh: Oliver and Boyd, 1969.
115. "To Whom It May Concern." *CLM*, 31 (1945): 61.

INTERVIEWS

1961

116. Lask, Thomas. "Dramatist in a Troubled World." *NYT,* 22 Jan. 1961, sec. 2, p. 1.

    Albee discusses *AD*'s theme, the cause of artistic malaise, contemporary influences on the theater, how *ZS* got produced in Germany, his preference for writing one-act plays, and his educational background.

1962

117. Zindel, Paul and Loree Yerby. "Interview with Edward Albee." *Wagner Literary Magazine,* no. 3 (1962): 1–10.

    Albee comments on his dissatisfaction over the state of the theater, the function of a playwright to act as a social critic, the relation of musical structure and dramatic form, the use of profanity in drama as an "expletive," his writing habits, his reaction to the New York City Writers Conference, the use of Bessie Smith as a "catalyst" in *BS*, obtaining the rights to the adaptation of *SC*, his upcoming play *VW*, the duty of a theatrical agent, and *ZS*'s autobiographical overtones.

1963

118. Lask, Thomas. "Edward Albee at Ease." *NYT,* 27 Oct. 1963, sec. 2, p. 1.

    Albee's works in progress, his writing habits, and his adaptation of *SC* are featured.

119. "Soviet Writers Found Unafraid." *NYT,* 4 Dec. 1963, p. 54.

Albee discusses the attitude of Soviet authors and his views on Russian theater following a visit to Russia under the auspices of the State Department.

1965

120. Rutenberg, Michael E. "Two Interviews with Edward Albee," pp. 229–244. In *Edward Albee: Playwright in Protest*. New York: DBS, 1969.

The interview, which took place on 17 March 1965, features questions on play structure and musical form, character and staging aspects of *VW*, interpretation and the ending of *TA*, the fate of Grandma in *AD*, Carson McCullers's influence on *SC* and Albee's use of a black narrator, the absence of Bessie Smith in *BS*, the meaning of *SB* and its fate at the Spoleto Festival, the death scene and the characters in *ZS*, playwrighting functions and techniques, and American theater practices.

1966

121. Guernsey, Otis L. "Edward Albee Confronts Broadway, 1966." *Diplomat*, Oct. 1966, pp. 60–63.

Albee gives a description of *DB* and urges more critical tolerance and less "discrepancy between the value of a play and the notices it receives." He comments on critics, particulary Walter Kerr and Harold Clurman, and producer David Merrick. He provides his definition of comedy and applies it to *TA, M,* and *DB*. The movie and play of *VW* is discussed as well as the best American playwrights and new playwriting trends.

122. Lester, Elenore. "Albee: I'm Still in Process." *NYT*, 18 Sept. 1966, sec. 2, p. 1.

Albee along with co-producers Richard Barr and Clinton Wilder discuss the Albarwild Foundation and the type of play scripts received.

123. Newquist, Roy. "Interview with Edward Albee." In *Showcase*, pp. 129. New York: Morrow, 1966.

Albee is interviewed on his early years, his objective in playwriting, origins of his plays, critics' duties, the state of the American theater, *TA* and John Gielgud, securing the screen rights to *VW*, audience responsibility to the theater and the playwright, American theater heritage, repertory theaters, advice to potential playwrights, and his personal working habits with emphasis on revision.

1968

124. Rutenberg, Michael E. "Two Interviews with Edward Albee," pp. 244–260. In *Edward Albee: Playwright in Protest*. New York: DBS, 1969.

The 7 Aug. 1968 interview covers Albee's screenwriting in progress, musical structure and symbolism in *BM*, character motivation in *EG*, the theme of *DB*, character differences between the novel and stage adaptation of *M*, the title and idea for *TA*, homosexual implications and the child in *VW*, works in progress, critics, and his 1963 trip to Russia.

1969

125. Wardle, Irving. "Albee Looks at Himself and His Plays." *LT*, 18 Jan. 1969, p. 17.

Albee discusses directing his own plays eventually, his

adaptation *EG,* the overall structure of his plays, and the recurrence of animals in his plays.

1970

126. Clurman, Harold. *Ideas on the Theatre* [videotape]. New York: University at Large, Chelsea House, 1970. Clurman briefly interviews Albee on the tone of new scripts presented to the Playwright's Unit, the reason for realistic productions of Albee plays, and Albee's views on Broadway.

1971

127. Bosworth, Patricia. "Will They All Be Albees?" *NYT*, 18 July 1971, sec. 2, p. 1.

    Albee provides a tour of the William Flanagan Center for Creative Persons in Montauk, Long Island.

128. Diehl, Digby. "Edward Albee." In *Behind the Scenes,* edited by Joseph McCrindle, pp. 223–242. New York: Holt, Rinehart, and Winston, 1971.

    "Edward Albee Interviewed," *Transatlantic Review*, Summer 1963, pp. 57–72, is reprinted.

129. Flatley, Guy. "Edward Albee Fights Back." *NYT*, April 1971, sec. 2, p. 1. Reprinted in *NYTBE* 2 (April 1971): 1225–1227.

    Albee talks over the negative response to *AO,* New York critics, and the lack of an American theater culture, political theater, and serious theater. A brief biography on his partnership with Richard Barr is also featured. For letters to the editor on this interview, see "American Theater Dead or Alive?" *NYT,* 9 May 1971, sec. 2. p. 6.

130. Glover, William. "Albee: A Peep Within." *Houston Post Spotlight,* 25 April 1971, p. 21.

1974

131. Schneider, Howard. "Has the Tarantula Escaped?" *Pittsburgh Press,* 3 Feb. 1974. Reprinted in *Biography News,* (March 1974), pp. 246–247.

    Albee discusses SS, his early years, his underlying themes of politics and disengagement, his writing style, Americans' fear of experimentation, writing, and creativity.

132. "The Talk of the Town." *NY,* 3 June 1974, pp. 28–30.

    Interviewed by ninth graders, Albee talks on formulating an idea, his plays in foreign countries, Samuel Beckett, his control over his productions, his purpose in writing, and serious theater.

1975

133. "Albee: 'I Write to Unclutter My Mind.'" *NYT,* 26, Jan. 1975. p. 1.

    On the eve of the opening of SS, Albee reflects upon his working habits, the increase in public awareness, SS as fantasy, his writing as an act of optimism, and recurrence of basic themes in his works.

134. Gussow, Mel. "Recalling Evolution of *Seascape* Play, Albee Sees Tale Not of Lizard but of Life." *NYT,* 21 Jan. 1975, p. 40.

Albee discusses *SS*, particularly the research behind it, rejected ideas for it, and aspects of the production.

135. Sysa, Glenna. "'A Great Play Can Change the World.'" *Chicago Sun-Times,* 20 April 1975. Reprinted in *PA,* 28 (March-April 1975): D13–14.

    Albee notes the humor of his works, the lack of education in the arts, the social purpose of plays, "escapist fare in commercial theater," Joseph Papp, the disengagement of students, and his preference for "a play about national mentality" over "an agitprop play."

1976

136. "Edward Albee on Albee: The Superstar of Drama." *Boston Globe,* 14 March 1976. Reprinted in *NBPA,* 29 (March-April 1976): F7–8.

    Albee considers *AO* his best play, finds his work solid, speaks only of Beckett, and believes works today "lack economy" despite the abundance of talented new playwrights. He enjoys directing and plans to give *VW* a definitive production. A brief biography up to *ZS* is included.

137. Long, Mary. "Interview: Edward Albee." *Mademoiselle,* Aug. 1976, p. 230.

    Albee discusses his opposition to living false illusions, the purpose of his plays in exercising the truth, and the writer's function in society.

138. Oakes, Philip. "Don't Shoot the Playwright. . . ." *Sunday Times* (London), 12 Dec. 1976, p. 35.

    Albee's reaction to reviews in general, success, the

responsibility of an author, and the National Theatre production of *CW* are noted. He mentions his works in progress, his admiration for John Osborne, and his interest in musical structure as a dramatic form.

139. Stern, Daniel. "Albee: 'I Want My Intent Clear.'" *NYT*, 28 March 1976, sec. 2. p. 1.

    Albee comments on his direction of *VW* and his plans for giving it a definitive performance. Colleen Dewhurst and Ben Gazarra briefly discuss Albee's direction.

1977

140. Johnson, Malcolm L. "Albee at 48: Writing, Directing, Traveling, Thinking." *HC*, 23 Jan. 1977. Reprinted in *NBPA*, 11 (Jan.-Feb. 1977): B8–9.

    Albee recounts his plays in progress, his lifestyle, and his reasons for giving *CW* and *L* their American premiers at the Hartford Stage Company. The lack of serious theater on Broadway and the challenge of playwriting are discussed.

141. Von Ransom, Brooks. "Edward Albee Speaks." *Connecticut,* Feb. 1977, pp. 38–39.

    Albee canvasses his enjoyment of music, reading, and poetry, his dislike for screenwriting, his reason for premiering *CW* and *L* at the Hartford Stage Company, his impression of Hartford and his early years at Trinity College, and his ear for dialogue.

Secondary Sources

Secondary Sources

BIOGRAPHY

1961

142. Calta, Louis. "Stage Prize Won by Albee." *NYT*, 6 June 1961, p. 41.

    Albee wins the Lola D'Annunzio Award for his "sustained accomplishments in original playwriting."

143. "Theater Awards Scored." *NYT,* 30 June 1961, p. 30.

    AD and *BS* were named best plays of the 1960–1961 season by the Foreign Press Association. In a quote, Albee expresses anger for separate awards between Broadway and off-Broadway.

1963

144. "Albee Is Honored by Outer Circle." *NYT*, 1 May 1963, p. 34.

    Albee is cited as "the outstanding American playwright of the season." Alan Schneider, director of *VW*, and the cast are also honored.

145. "Albee to Do Libretto for Flanagan." *NYT*, 28 Aug. 1963, p. 38.

    Mike Flanagan and Edward Albee will collaborate on an original opera, *The Ice Age*. The article also notes their previous collaborations.

146. "Award Given to *Virginia Woolf*." *NYT*, 26 April 1963, p. 25.

    VW wins the Drama Critics' Circle Best Play Award for 1962–1963.

147. Calta, Louis. "Albee Leaving for Soviet to Join Steinbeck in Cultural Exchange." *NYT*, 1 Nov. 1963, p. 28.

    Albee will lead group discussions in Russia, Poland, Hungary, and Czechoslovakia under the auspices of the State Department's cultural exchange program.

148. Tanner, Henry. "Steinbeck and Albee Speak Out in Soviet for U.S. Professor." *NYT*, 15 Nov. 1963, p. 1.

    The two authors condemn the arrest of Yale Professor Frederick C. Barghoorn during their cultural foreign exchange tour.

149. "*Virginia Woolf* Is Named Best Play of the Year." *NYT*, 29 April 1963, p. 25.

    The play receives the Tony Award along with Uta Hagen (Best Actress), George Hill (Best Actor), Richard Schneider (Best Director), and Richard Barr and Clinton Wilder (Best Producers).

150. Zolotow, Sam. "Playwrights Get a New Workshop." *NYT*, 13 Nov. 1963, p. 34.

Albee, Richard Barr, and Clinton Wilder establish the Playwright's Unit Workshop with profits from *VW*.

1964

151. Moritz, Charles, ed. *Current Biography Yearbook*, pp. 1–3. New York: Wilson, 1964.

The biography recounts Albee's family, education, youth, play-writing career and criticism up to *VW*, and his philosophy. A personal evaluation and address of his agent is included.

152. Stambusky, Alan A. "Continuing Trends in U.S. College and University and Play Selection, 1962–63." *ETJ*, 16 (May 1964): 160–166.

Four hundred fifty-five replies from college and university members of the American Educational Theater Association ranks Albee as the second most-produced Absurdist.

1965

153. "American Actors Criticized." *LT*, 2 Jan. 1965, p. 6.

Albee is criticized by Actor's Equity for casting English actors in *TA*. Albee finds their resentment "rather silly."

154. "Villanova and Theater '65 Win Margo Jones Awards." *NYT*, 16 Feb. 1965, p. 40.

Albee, Clinton Wilder, and Richard Barr, co-founders of Theater '65 are honored for their encouragement of young playwrights.

1966

155. Rigdon, Walter, ed. *The Biographical Encyclopedia and Who's Who of the American Theatre,* p. 236. New York: Heineman, 1966.

    The biography includes Albee's parents, education, membership, address, plays up to *SC* including dates of first productions, and awards received.

156. Stambusky, Alan A. "The 'America First' Attitude in U.S. College and University Play Selection, a Five Year Report." *ETJ,* 18 (May 1966): 136–139.

    Albee is the third most-produced playwright of 1964–1965 according to responses from 567 members of the American Educational Theater Association.

157. Zolotow, Sam. "Albee Rewriting *Holly* Libretto." *NYT,* 14 Nov. 1966, p. 52.

    Albee replaces Abe Burrows in rewriting *Holly Golightly,* a musical based on Truman Capote's novel *Breakfast at Tiffany's.*

1967

158. Hartnoll, Phyllis, ed. *The Oxford Companion to the Theater,* p. 17. London: Oxford University Press, 1967.

    Albee's plays up to *TA* are listed with producers and premier productions. A history of his foster father is included.

159. Toohey, John L. *A History of the Pulitzer Prize Plays,* pp. 334–339. New York: Citadel, 1967.

A recapitulation of Albee's career, a synopsis of critical notices on the Broadway production of *DB*, and Albee's statement following the Pulitzer Prize Award for 1966 are featured.

1968

160. Ballew, Leighton M. and Gerald Kahan. "Production Trends in the American College and University Theatres: Problems and Perspectives." *ETJ*, 20 (Oct. 1968): 449–456.

    In the American Educational Theater Association Production Survey, Albee is second in 1965 and first in 1966 in the category of Most Frequently Produced Playwrights (One-Acts). He is second in 1965–1966 and 1966–1967 as the Most Frequently Produced Playwright (All Categories).

161. "Play Plan Grows into Arts Center." *NYT*, 16 Jan. 1968, p. 1.

    Albee, Richard Barr, and Clinton Wilder plan to establish a nonprofit performing arts center on Broadway. A tentative list of plays is provided.

1969

162. Funke, Lewis. "West Coast *Tiny Alice* Passes Albee's Scrutiny Here." *NYT*, 29 Sept. 1969, p. 52.

    Albee requested to see the ACT production in San Francisco after rumors of "transposition of scenes, alterations in text and offbeat interpretations of several characters."

163. Harte, Barbara and Carolyn Riley, eds. *Contemporary*

Authors, pp. 18–20, rev. ed. Vol. 5–8. Detroit: Gale, 1969.

The biography recounts his personal life, career, writings up to *BM*, philosophy, and influences. A list of biographical/critical sources is included.

164. ———. *200 Contemporary Authors*, pp. 17–20. New York: Gale, 1969.

    The biography is divided into Personal (Parents, education, religion, home, and agent), Writings up to *BM* with premier performances, Sidelights (Critical opinion, interviews on his plays, and writing styles), Advocational Interests, and Biographical/Critical Sources, 1961–1968.

165. Popkin, Henry. "Edward Albee." In *Reader's Encyclopedia of World Drama*, pp. 10–12. Edited by John Gassner and Edward Quinn. New York: Crowell, 1969.

    A short biography of Albee is included with brief interpretations of his plays up to *BM*.

166. Weiler, A.H. "Albee to Adapt French Novel to Film." *NYT*, 24 April 1969, p. 38.

    Roland Topor's *The Tenant* will be adapted for Universal Pictures. Albee and Richard Barr's Theater 1970 Film Productions will co-produce.

1970

167. Gross, Theodore. "Edward Albee." In *Representative Men*, pp. 284–285. New York: Free Press, 1970.

The biography recounts his early years and lists his plays up to *DB*. Gross finds his "harsh cynicism" distinctively different from O'Neill, Williams, and Miller. A reprint of Henry Knepler's "Edward Albee: Conflict of Tradition" (*MD*, 10 [Dec. 1967]: 274–279) follows.

168. Weiler, A. H. "Who's Afraid of Vaslav Nijinsky?" *NYT*, 29 March 1970, sec. 2, p. 15.

Albee will write the screenplay *The Dancer* based upon the Russian ballet artist.

1971

169. Ballew, Leighton and Gerald Kahan. "The AETA Production Lists Project Survey: 1969–1970." *ETJ*, 23 (Oct. 1971): 298–306.

The American Educational Theater Association Survey lists Albee ninth as the Most Frequently Produced Playwright (full-length), first in the one-act category and third in all categories. *VW* is the fifth most-produced full length play. *ZS* is first, *AD* is fourth, and *SB* is seventh in the one-act category.

170. Nemy, Enid. "Benefit Party for Playwrights Unit Held After Opening." *NYT*, 29 March 1971, p. 29.

The party held after the opening of *AO* features comments by Mrs. Reed Albee about her foster son and the play.

1972

171. Matlaw, Myron. *Modern World Drama: An Encylopedia*, pp. 16–17. New York: Dutton, 1972.

Albee's early years, a synopsis of his plays up to *AO*, critical reactions, themes, techniques, and a selective bibliography are offered.

172. Witman, Alden. "Albee to Direct in Hamptons." *NYT*, 26 March 1972, sec. 15, p. 1. Reprinted in *NYTBE* 3 (March 1972): 455–456.

    Albee plans to direct the John Drew Summer Theater in East Hampton, Long Island for eight weeks. One of the plays sceduled is *AD* with the original cast.

173. *Who's Who in the Theater*, pp. 446–447, 15th ed.; rev. London: Pitman, 1972.

    The biography lists schools attended, plays written up to *AO*, plays directed and produced, and awards and honors received.

1973

174. Bigsby, C.W.E. "Edward Albee." In *Contemporary Dramatists*, edited by James Vinson, pp. 23–26. New York: St. Martin's and London: St. James, 1973.
    The biography lists the author's educational background, places employed and duties, an extensive list of honors received, initial production dates of *ZS* to *AO* in England and America and gives brief criticism of plays up to *AO* with emphasis on *VW, TA, DB, BM*, and *AO*.

175. *Who's Who in the World*, p. 15, 2d ed.; rev. Chicago: Marquis, 1973.

    Albee's birth date, plays written up to *AO*, membership, and address of agent are listed.

1975

176. "ACT–Albee Feud Goes On—So Does the Play." *SFE*, 21 Oct. 1975. Reprinted in *NBPA*, 84 (Nov.–Dec. 1975): C9.

    Director William Ball refuses to comply with Albee's wishes concerning a production of *TA;* therefore, the William Morris Agency has demanded that the original text must be followed or the show must cease.

177. "Albee Hasn't Sued Yet." *OT*, 9 Oct. 1975. Reprinted in *NBPA*, 84 (Nov.–Dec. 1975): C12.

    Executive producer of American Conservatory Theater plans to meet with Albee's representatives to settle the dispute over William Ball's production of *TA*.

178. "Albee vs. Ball—Continued." *SFE*, 28 Oct. 1975. Reprinted in *NBPA*, 84 (Nov.–Dec. 1975): C10.

    Samuel French, Inc. denounces ACT's production as "unauthorized" and "a violation of Edward Albee's rights." The play, however, will continue.

179. "Director Rebuffs Playwright." *OT*, 7 Oct. 1975. Reprinted in *NBPA*, 68 (Sept.-Oct. 1975): D9.

    Albee has condemned the San Francisco American Conservatory Theater production of *TA*, but has allowed the play to continue only for the actors' benefit. A lawsuit is rumored.

180. Eichelbaum, Stanley, "Albee vs. Ball—Act II." *SFE*, 7 Oct. 1975. Reprinted in *NBPA, 84,* (Nov.-Dec. 1975): C11.

Albee calls the San Francisco ACT production a "disgrace" and vows to stop the play. He is tired of Ball's tampering with the script for the third time since 1964.

181. "New York Intelligencer." *NYM,* 10 Feb. 1975, p. 57.

A new Edward Albee television play, *Talk Show,* modeled on a real talk show, is making the rounds at the networks.

182. Schwartz, Jerry. "Government Subsidies Needed for Theater, Panel Members Say." *Miami Herald,* 16 March 1975. Reprinted in *NBPA,* 31 (March-April 1975): E6.

Albee, Clive Barnes, George Rose, and Tammy Grimes discuss the need for government to support serious theater. The forum was held by the Society of Four Arts in Miami.

1976

183. Ballew, Leighton M. "The UCTA Production Lists Project Survey—1973–74: 'The Good Old Bad Old Plays'—Again?" *ETJ,* 28 (March 1976): 97–105.

Replies from 448 colleges and universities place Albee fourth in one-act dramatists and 15th most frequently produced in all categories. *ZS* is the third most frequently produced one-act and *AD* is seventh.

184. Lester, Elenore. "Where Have All the Playwrights Gone?" *NYT,* 22 Aug. 1976, sec. 2, p. 1.

The article studies the fate of Jack Richardson, Arthur Kopit, Jack Gelber, and Albee. Albee "has failed to achieve that dynamic ongoing relationship which exists between a major playwright and his audience." Like his contemporaries, his theme of "preservation of the individual from the mass" has become outmoded.

185. *Who's Who in America*, p. 30, 39th ed.; rev. Volume 1. Chicago: Marquis, 1976.

    Birth date, a list of plays up to SS, offices held, and mailing address of Albee are listed.

1977

186. *International Who's Who*, p. 21-22, 41st ed.; rev. London: Europa, 1977.

    The Albee entry lists his occupation, birth date, education, plays up to CW, and the address of his agent.

187. *Who's Who*, p. 22, 129th ed.; rev. New York: St. Martin's, 1977.

    The reference lists Albee's plays up to CW and L, occupation, birth date, and mailing address.

CRITICISM

1961

188. Grebanier, Bernard. *Playwriting*, pp. 123-138. New York: Crowell, 1961.

    Albee uses the bench and knife in ZS as a third personality—a necessity in a two-character play. An excerpt from the end of ZS is included.

189. "New Yorkers Crowd to New American Satire." *LT*, 10 April 1961, p. 3.

In the Off-Broadway productions of *ZS, AD,* and *BS,* Albee "comments tartly upon our more conventional conformist citizens." *ZS* recalls Samuel Beckett with "American elements."*AD* is akin to Ionesco and Beckett, but thinner in texture. *BS* is stylized "Broadway realism" but still shows signs of experimentation. The cast is good.

190. Tallmer, Jerry. "Theater: *The American Dream.*" *VV*, 2 Feb. 1961, p. 11.

The play is "a hilarious dirty joke, wafted through and through with *essence* of inversion and *eau de* necrophilia." The opening is reminiscent of *The Bald Soprano*. The dialogue is "neat and sharp" and Albee attacks many areas. "The production . . . was close to perfect." *B* "is sorry gruel."

191. Tallmer, Jerry. "Theater: *The Death of Bessie Smith.*" *VV*, 9 March 1961, p. 9

The play is an "acidulous study of the species Womankind in its manifestion of intolerable neurotic bitch." Rae Allen "makes the lady lively enough and handsome enough" and the remainder of the cast is "adequate or better." Direction by Lawrence Arrick "has some halting moments and William Flanagan's music is of par."

192. Taubman, Howard. "The Theater: Offerings for Latin Tour."*NYT*, 19 July 1961, p. 26.

ZS is one of the plays that will tour Latin America under the auspices of the New York Repertory Company. The play "has artistic integrity," and "honors, rather than disgraces the United States."

193. "Well of Bitter Laughter." *LT*, 25 Oct. 1961, p. 13.

Albee "sketches in with brilliant strokes his impression of a modern girl's neurosis" in *BS*. "Mr. Albee is a great hater and almost as inventive as M. Ionesco" in *AD*. Both plays were performed at the Royal Court Theatre, London.

1962

194. Duprey, Richard. *Just Off the Aisle: The Ramblings of a Catholic Critic*, pp. 75–80, Westminister, Md.: Newman, 1962.

Albee is an avant gardist who "has an axe to grind" and "is too busy indulging in private ironies to share with the humble generation that is inevitably present in an artist who is earnest and true." The faults of *ZS*, *BS*, and *SB* are discussed.

1963

195. "Albee Play Seen by Few Africans." *NYT*, 24 Sept. 1963, p. 45.

Despite desegregated audiences, many nonwhites are unable to see the South African touring company production of *VW*. Reactions to the play by South Africans are offered.

196. Cavarozzi, Joyce Pennington. "An Analysis of the Plays of Edward Albee." M.A. thesis, Ohio State University, 1963.

197. "Edward Albee Dramatizes Carson McCullers." *LT*, 25 Nov. 1963, p. 15.

SC is "still primarily a story and not a drama." Amelia's character is foreshadowed by *VW* and *BS*. Principle characters are lacking though performances attempt to compensate. The narrator is a mistake and his speeches come across too literary. The fight scene is "well done."

198. Jansky, Ann Leah. "Formless Form in the Plays of Edward Albee." M.A. thesis, St. Louis University, 1963.

199. "1000 in South Africa Wait in Vain to See Albee's Play." *NYT*, 3 Oct. 1963, p. 31.

VW is halted by censors in Johannesburg.

200. *"Who's Afraid of Virginia Woolf?" New Mexico Quarterly Review*, 33 (Winter 1963–1964): 465–466.

The original cast recording is as effective as seeing the play because it "is a play of words rather than action. . . ."

1964

201. "Advanced Tactics in Marital Warfare." *LT*, 7 Feb. 1964, p. 15.

American "kidding" and language used as a "flexible and sophisticated instrument" aid *VW's* "ironic comment on the chaos of current social values." Despite the faulty child-myth, the play is "a major American work" akin to O'Neill. Alan Schneider's direction and

Uta Hagen's acting as Martha are commendable.

202. Bristow, Donald Gene. "New Voice in the Theatre: A Structural and Thematic Analysis of the Plays of Edward Albee." M.F.A. thesis, University of Oklahoma, 1964.

203. *Choice: Review of Books,* 1 (May 1964): 103.

    The love triangle and "passages on the mystery of love" suffer in the adaptation of *SC*. The play is valuable, however, in a "comparison-contrast study with the novella."

204. Hankiss, Elmer. "Who's Afraid of Edward Albee?" *New Hungarian Quarterly,* 5 (Autumn 1964): 168–174.

    VW is an avant gardist piece which constitutes a successful protest. The protest lies within "the struggle fought by the two leading characters against the senselessness of life." The game motif emphasizes their "vacuum."

205. Jones, Donna Mae. "The Drama of Edward Albee: An Analytical Study of His Life and Works." M.A. thesis, University of Wisconsin, 1964.

206 Lauricella, James. "A Director's Journal for the Production of Two One-Act Plays: Edward Albee's *The Zoo Story* and Samuel Beckett's *Krapp's Last Tape*. M.F.A. thesis, Ohio University, 1964.

207. Morse, Ben. "Three Ballads." *P*, Feb. 1964, p. 138.

    Albee "has somewhat fallen short of the essence of the original" in the Broadway production of *SC*. The characters "lose rather than gain in dimension." The set and lighting detract from the overall effect.

208. Solomon, Jerry. "Edward Albee: American Absurdist?" *Western Speech,* 28 (Fall 1964): 230–236.

Albee is "intensely individual, adamantly social, and devastatingly satirical—and the latter two qualities make it almost impossible for him to fit into the Absurd mold." His existential philosophy is more akin to Albert Camus than Beckett and Ionesco: "For Camus, and for Albee, the recognition of the Absurd paradox is not the end process. Man must continually reassert his own humanistic individuality in order to become, indeed a man."

209. Stace, Ann Carolyn. "An Analysis and Criticism of the World of Edward Albee." M.A. thesis, Miami University (Ohio), 1964.

210. Ulanov, Barry. "Brecht and Albee." *Catholic World*, Jan. 1964, pp. 263–264.

The Broadway production of *SC* is a pointless and bad adaptation plagued by inconsistent accents, ill-defined characters, and a cloudy situation.

211. Wines, Mildred Hale. "Origins of the Major Elements of the Theatre of the Absurd with Reference to the Works of Albee, Gelbert, and Kopit." M.A. thesis, Catholic University, 1964.

1965

212. Cahn, Judah. *"Tiny Alice." Reconstructionist,* 14 May 1965, pp. 22–27.

TA "is not so much a study of symbolism as it is a symptom of great sickness, of hopelessness, of utter frustration with which many young people are afflicted and with which we must reckon." The characters do not fight their dilemma, and Julian's purposeless death masks as martyrdom.

213. Calta, Louis. "Beckett and Albee Back in Double Bill." *NYT*, 9 June 1965, p. 42.

   The Cherry Lane Theater revival of *ZS* is commendable, particularly acting by Ben Piazza and George Bartenieff.

214. Chiari, J. *Landmarks of Contemporary Drama*, pp. 158–160. London: Jenkins, 1965.

   VW has "dazzling" dialogue and "dramatic skill," but the characters offer little sympathy, and the play is a series of contrived events that lack dramatic growth.

215. Ellison, Jerome. "God on Broadway: Deity as Reflected in the Work of Seven Playwrights Prominent in the Twentieth Century American Commerical Theater: O'Neill, Wilder, MacLeish, Williams, Miller, Albee, Chayefski." M.A. thesis, Southern Connecticut State College, 1965–1966.

216. Hurley, Paul J. "France and America: Versions of the Absurd." *College English,* 26 (May 1965): 634–640.

   Albee's version of absurdism differs from the French attitude because he moralizes in *AD* and exposes social harms through conventional social realism in *BS* and *VW*.

217. Rutenberg, Michael Elliot. "Edward Albee: Social Critic." Ph.D. dissertation, Yale University, 1965.

218. "Taut Rhythms of Albee." *LT*, 29 June 1965, p. 8.

The Granada television production of *BS* lacks "intellectual content." Albee's writing skill, however, makes the proceedings "vividly theatrical." Cast and direction are commendable.

219. Terrien, Samuel. "Albee's Alice." *Christianity and Crisis*, 28 June 1965, pp. 140–143.

TA "seeks to revive without dishonesty the theatre of communion" through a mixture of Lewis Carroll fantasy, mythology, Christianity, and Freudian concepts.

1966

220. Anzalone, Frank Michael. "The Relation of Love and Death in the Plays of Edward Albee." M.A. thesis, Catholic University, 1966.

221. Brustein, Robert. "The New American Playwrights." In *Modern Occasions*, edited by Philip Rahv, pp. 123–218. New York: Farrar, 1966.

Allbee is evaluated on pp. 124–127. He is theatrical "both through words and striking visual images." He frequently borrows from others, however, for technique because he lacks "the power to penetrate a subject deeply. . . ." Sexual pathology is common to all his plays.

222. Canaday, Nicholas. "Albee's *The American Dream* and the Existential Vacuum." *South Central Bulletin*, 26 (Winter 1966): 28–34.

AD "mirrors the meaninglessness of American life." Positive values, however are reinforced through Grandma who promotes "courageous realism" as a means of maintaining human dignity.

223. Crowther, Bosley. "Who's Afraid of Audacity?" *NYT*, 10 July 1966, sec. 2, p. 10. Reprinted in *NYTFR*, pp. 3621–3622. Volume 5. New York: New York Times and Arno Press, 1970.

 The film version of *VW*, "an artful truncation of the play or a subtle bowdlerization of Mr. Albee's play," clears up many obscurities and leaves the impression that the games are commonplace.

224. "Dramatic Decline." *TLS*, 26 May 1966, p. 472.

 A review of the book labels *TA* as "a disconnected series of shock tactics combining cultural pretension with a gloating appetite for cruelty."

225. Kauffman, Stanley. "Screen: Funless Games at George and Martha's." *NYT*, 24 June 1966, p. 28. Reprinted in *NYTFR*, p. 3620, New York: New York Times and Arno Press, 1970.

226. Kelly, Edward. "Dominant Recurring Themes in the Published Plays of Edward Albee." M.A. thesis, Kent State University, 1966.

227. Kerr, Walter. "Only Time Really Happens to People." *NYT*, 2 Oct, 1966, sec. 2, p. 1.

 Albee implies in *DB* "that words can be fitted together well enough but that the moment they are all substance vanishes." Setting and direction of the Broadway production are effective. The chief fault lies in the dialogue which makes the play "speculative rather than theatrical."

228. Kitchin, Laurence. *Drama in the Sixties: Form and Interpretation*, pp. 196–198. London: Faber, 1966.

    ZS and BS are based upon "misapplied psychology," "brainwashing," and conflicting characters, one of whom dominates. VW is more successful due to its "two dominant malicious characters" and "comedy of manners" style.

229. Laufe, Abe. *Anatomy of a Hit: Long Run Plays on Broadway from 1900 to the Present Day*, pp. 302–308. New York: Hawthorn, 1966.

    A recapitulation of the Broadway production of VW is offered: critical opinion, honors received, and profits made. The reasons for its long run are "morbid fascination" and "excellent critical reviews."

230. McMurrian, Jaqueline Y. "Edward Albee: Absurdist for Social Reform." M.A. thesis, University of Maryland, 1966.

231. Pearre, Howard. "How to Be Graceful with Noblesse Oblige," *NashB*, 2 Dec. 1966, p. 36.

    The book review cites DB as "Albee's best work to date with the possible exception of *Tiny Alice*." His "maturity" is "outstanding."

232. Sullivan, Dan. "Ill-fated *Breakfast at Tiffany's*." *NYT*, 15 Dec. 1966, p. 60.

    Edward Albee's libretto is "an exercise in the Pirandello style about fiction and reality."

233. Thompson, Howard. "Albee's *A Delicate Balance* Goes into Rehearsal." *NYT*, 16 Aug. 1966, p. 35.

Albee holds the first rehearsal in his Greenwich Village home. The play is briefly discussed.

1967

234. Albee's *A Delicate Balance* Praised in Paris Opening." *NYT*, 28 Oct. 1967, p. 35.

France-soir newspaper found the performances "dazzling," though questioned the text. The production was performed at the Théâtre de France.

235. Bigsby, C.W.E. *Confrontation and Committment: A Study of Contemporary American Drama, 1959-1966*, pp. 71–92. Kansas City: University of Missouri Press, 1967.

In Albee's plays, "the self is seen as a barrier between the individual and the rest of humanity." He proposes confrontation in ZS, exposes a corrupt society through European absurdism in *AD*, and displays the destruction of false illusions in *DB* and *VW*. Albee dismisses religion as a substitute of confrontation in *TA*, and uses *M* to express a "sense of alienation from the empty and bizarre world of modern society."

236. Boros, Donald. "*Tiny Alice* by Edward Albee: A Production Record and Analysis with Emphasis on Dynamic Theatrical Symbolism." M. A. thesis, Saint Cloud State College (Minnesota), 1967.

237. Callahan, J. Stephen. "Society, Sex, and Soul in the

Plays of Edward Albee." M.A. thesis, University of Kansas, 1967.

238. Cohen, Marshall. "Theater '67." *Partisan Review*, 34 (Summer 1967): 436–444.

A review of the Broadway production on pp. 442–443 labels *DB* an imperfect imitation of T. S. Eliot. The balance "is overly explicit and dramatically redundant." The play is built around "Get the Guests," "exhausted imagery and grammatical perversities."

239. Downer, Alan S. "The Doctor's Dilemma: Notes on the New York Theatre, 1966–1967." *QJS*, 53 (Oct. 1967): 220–221.

In the Broadway production of *DB*, the "family was written and played with such skill as to retain for Albee his appointment as the somewhat desperate hope of the American theatre."

240. Duprey, Richard A. "Today's Dramatists." In *American Theatre*, Stratford-Upon-Avon Studies, no. 10, pp. 209–224, New York: St. Martin's Press and London: Arnold, 1967.

Albee's writing style is "eclectic" and views life pessimistically. He employs absurdism in *ZS*, *AD*, and *SB*; realism in *BS*; and naturalism in *VW*. The failure of *SC* is due to its odd assortment of characters. *TA* diminishes in quality after the opening scene. Overall, Albee is a "theatricalist" who writes for selfish reasons.

241. Ellis, Donald. "Edward Albee: A Critical Reception Study." M.A. thesis, University of Kansas, 1967.

242. Fitzgerald, J. "Edward Albee: Growing into Great-

ness?" *Ave Maria* (Notre Dame), 7 June 1967, pp. 7–9.

Though *DB* lacks depth, the Broadway production is witty and more substantial than his previous plays. The plot is thin and the language never rises "to the level of pure poetry." The play, however, "shows evidence of such growing maturity and offers hope of better things to come." Cast and direction are commendable.

243. Fletcher, William D. "An Analysis of the Women Characters in Six of Edward Albee's Plays." M.A. thesis, Indiana University, 1967.

244. Freedman, Morris. *The Moral Impulse: Modern Drama from Ibsen to the Present*, pp. 122–124. Carbondale: Southern Illinois University Press, 1967.

Albee's absurdism in *ZS*, *AD*, *SB*, and *VW* employs psychology. "He takes truth implicit in a situation to its inevitable and consequently, always absurd conclusion. . . ."

245. French, Paul Douglas. "The Struggle with Forms and the Search for Theme in the Plays of Edward Albee." Ph.D. dissertation, Loyola University of Chicago, 1967.

246. Hobson, Harold. "A Dazzling Parisian Cast in *Delicate Balance*." *CSM*, 6 Nov. 1967, p. 6.

The Jean-Louis Barrault production at the Odéon Theater in Paris boasts "the most remarkable cast," costumes by Yves St. Laurent, and an alleviation from Albee's theme of "unutterable despair."

247. Johnson, Martha J. "Note on a Possible Source for

Who's Afraid of Virginia Woolf?" Radford Review, 21 (1967): 231–233.

Virginia Woolf's short story "Lappin and Lapinova" and Albee's *VW* are thematically similar. Both couples—George and Martha and Ernest and Rosalind—have developed a fantasy world to avoid reality. The men end the game by reasserting their superiority, thus leaving both women "with an unfilled void—alone, broken, and humbled."

248. Levine, Mordecai H. "Albee's Liebestod." *CLA*, 10 (March 1967): 252–255.

Religious interpretations reveal Jerry and Peter in *ZS* as Jeremiah the Prophet and Peter the Disciple, respectively. Sociologically, Jerry is the outcast ignored by the upper class. Psychologically, Jerry can only find "gratification and love" by sharing his physical pain with Peter.

249. Matthews, Honor. *The Primal Curse*, pp. 201–205. London: Chatto, 1967.

In *ZS*, "the [Cain and Abel] myth is twisted, for the aggressor [Jerry] throws down the knife at his victim's feet and . . . achieves before death a transient fulfilment and peace." Martha in *VW* is also an aggressor who is destroyed by the weaker (George) through a weapon—an imaginary son.

250. Olin, Carol. "The Unique Style of Edward Albee: Creative Uses of the Past." M.A. thesis, University of Colorado, 1967.

251. Palazzo, Laura. "A Comparative Study of the Plays of Edward Albee." M.A. thesis, Syracuse University, 1967.

252. Parsatharathy, R. "Who's Afraid of Edward Albee? (American Drama of the Sixties)." *Quest*, 55 (Autumn 1967): 53–55.

Albee began new American theater at a time European Absurd theater was influential and American playwrights (Williams, Miller, and Inge) were being rejected. Albee's plays display emotionality rather than intellect. Thus, his language and imagination outweigh his vision.

253. Paul, Louis. "A Game Analysis of Albee's *Who's Afraid of Virginia Woolf?:* The Core of Grief." *Literature and Psychology*, 17 (1967): 47–51.

Martha and George play games similar to Berne's definition in *Games People Play* to avoid grief and make contact with each other.

254. Tynan, Kenneth. *Tynan Right and Left*, pp. 135–136. New York: Atheneum, 1967.

A review of the 1963 Broadway production of *VW* finds the child gimmickry and the humanism-verses-science debate questionable. Uta Hagen and Arthur Hill are good as George and Martha, but the script is too amusing to be moving. The theme of impotence is typical of today's plays.

255. Way, Brian. "Albee and the Absurd: *The American Dream* and *The Zoo Story*." In *American Theatre*. Stratford-Upon-Avon Studies, no. 10., pp. 188–207. New York: St. Martin's Press and London: Arnold, 1967.

Like Ionesco, Albee attacks "conventions of social behavior." *ZS* and *AD* deal with the evils of "human isolation." Albee employs the absurdist characteristic of "devaluation of language." Unlike the European absurdist plays, *ZS* and *AD* have "tightly wrapped up" denouements and attempt to prove a point rather than make a statement on the human condition.

1968

256. Bannon, Barbara A. *PW,* 5 Feb. 1968, p. 62.

    The book review of *EG* states that "This may well not be the best of Albee adaptations, or approach his own original plays in forcefulness, but it has the scratchy emotions, the horror-behind-the-polite-calm, which are Albee trademarks."

257. Barnes, Clive. "Theatre: Edward Albee Takes Adventurous Step." *NYT,* 8 March 1968, p. 48.

    BM, in its premiere at the Buffalo Studio Arena Theater, "may well be one of Albee's best plays; it is unquestionably his most adventurous." The absence of narrative is unique in American theater. The actors "provide an admirable vocal and emotional balance." Direction by Alan Schneider and set by William Ritman make the premiere "authoritative and convincing."

258. ———. "The Theater: *Krapp's Last Tape* and *Zoo Story.*" *NYT,* 11 Oct. 1968, p. 41.

    The revival by Theater 1969 Playwrights Repertory at the Billy Rose Theater has commendable direction by Richard Barr and acting by Ben Piazza and Donald Davis. Though the end of *ZS* is flawed, "the writing is beautiful."

259. Bigsby, C.W.E. "Strategy of Madness: An Analysis of Edward Albee's *A Delicate Balance.*" *Contemporary*

Literature, 9 (13 April 1968): 223-235. Reprinted in *Albee,* pp. 96-109. Edinburgh: Oliver and Boyd, 1969.

The situation, characters, and effectiveness of the play are discussed as well as Albee's overall intent.

260. Bourdonnay, Katherine. "The Use of Violence and Hostility as a Means of Communication in the Original Plays of Edward Albee." M.A. thesis, Catholic University, 1968.

261. Burns, Carolyn Dolinich. "The Function of the Narrator in Contemporary American Drama from Wilder to Albee." M.A. thesis, Catholic University, 1968.

262. Campbell, Mary Elizabeth. "The Statement of Edward Albee's *Tiny Alice.*" *Papers on Language and Literature,* 4 (Winter 1968): 85-100.

TA is an allegorical statement on materialism. The model is literally a symbol of unfeeling technological power. Tiny Alice is figuratively the wealth that allures, then ruins the lives of men.

263. Chapman, John. "Albee's *Box-Mao-Box* Built with Monologues." *NYDN,* 1 Oct. 1968. Reprinted in *NYTCR,* 1968, pp. 228-289.

The play consists of five monologues and little movement. *Box* is difficult to comprehend and no attempt is made at meaning in *Mao.*

264. Cook, Bruce. "*Box-Mao-Box:* Parts for Do-It-Yourself Drama."*NO,* 7 Oct. 1968, p. 22.

The play "is clearly intended to annoy" and "is not truly exciting."

265. Cooke, Richard P. "The Theater." *WSJ*, 2 Oct. 1968. Reprinted in *NYTCR*, 1968, pp. 229-230.

Albee's musical structure is less evident in *Box* than in *Mao*. Mao's elusiveness is "irritating." Albee never allows audience sympathy for his characters. The evening is for unconventional theater-goers who are "primarily inquisitive."

266. Curry, Ryder H. and Michael Porte. "The Surprising Unconscious of Edward Albee." *DS*, 7 (Winter 1968-1969): 59-68.

"*Tiny Alice* is, in dramatic form, a demonstration of a psychic transformation in line with Newton's metaphysical (minor thesis), and a Gnostic rite of release (major thesis)." Albee's "double mystery" is proven through an analysis of action, characters, and dialogue in light of Gnostic rites.

267. "The Theater." *T*, 11 Oct. 1968, p. 73.

BM is another example of "the alarming deterioration of a formidable talent." The play deliberately lacks a plot line and the characters' monologues possess "no visible thematic length. . . . " Albee's attempt at musical structure fails.

268. Dillon, Perry Claude. "The Characteristics of the French Theatre of the Absurd in the Plays of Edward Albee and Harold Pinter." Ph.D. dissertation, University of Arkansas, 1968. Abstracted in *DA*, 29 (1968): 257-258A.

The study examines *ZS*, *SB*, *AD*, *VW*, *TA*, and *DB* for elements of French absurdism. Concern for language and themes are the two elements Albee has most in common with French absurdists.

269. Forbes, Anthony. "New Play Advances Albee's Reputation." *NashB*, 26 April 1968, p. 28.

The book review of *EG* labels it a major work "whichadvances Albee as one of the two or three top dramatists in the world today."

270. Gassner, John. *Dramatic Soundings: Evaluations and Retractions Culled from Thirty Years of Dramatic Criticism*, pp. 591-607. New York: Crown, 1968.

Reprints of theater reviews of *AD* and *BS* (May 1961), *VW* (March and 29 June 1963), *SC* (March 1964), *TA* (Oct. 1965), and *DB* (Dec. 1966) are offered.

271. Gill, Brendan. "The Theatre." *NY*, 12 Oct. 1968, pp. 103-104.

BM has "ancient familiar themes of death, art, and time," lack of action, cliché-ridden dialogue. The result is a "delightful evening." The cast is commendable.

272. Gottfried, Martin. "Theatre." *WWD*, 1 Oct. 1968. Reprinted in *NYTCR*, 1968, p. 230.

BM "is sloppy, boring, and, frankly, stupid." Both plays are self-indulgent and superficially influenced by "Samuel Beckett's antiphysicality." Ruth White is the only standout in the cast. Direction and set are faulty.

273. Gottfried, Martin. *A Theater Divided: The Postwar American Stage*, pp. 264-274. Boston: Little, Brown, 1968.

ZS, like *SB*, *AD*, *VW*, *SC*, *TA*, *M*, and *DB* "is weak in theory, strong in drama, runs away from its author and has no stylistic relationship to any of his work except for a self-consciousness in the use of language." Homosexuality, dominant-mother, passive-father, and son figures pervade his work. *TA* is his most honest work; its effectiveness was realized more so in the ACT production than the Broadway production.

274. Halperen, Max. "What Happens in *Who's Afraid . . . ?*" In *Modern American Drama: Essays in Criticism*, edited by William E. Taylor, pp. 129-143. Deland, Fla.: Everett/Edwards, 1968.

   Man must rebel against social and economic pressures if he is to become whole in *ZS*, *AD*, *BS*, and *VW*. The ability to love and communicate comes through an "explosion." This point does not develop fully in *VW* because of 1) scenes that do not play simultaneously on an intellectual and emotional level, 2) meaningless dialogue, and 3) the child symbol.

275. Hamblen, Abigail Ann. "Edward Albee . . . and the Fear of Virginia Woolf." *Trace* 2 (1968): 198-203.

   Both *VW* and the works of Virginia Woolf deal with "the essential loneliness and suffering of individuals and of the pain of heightened perceptiveness. . . ."

276. Harris, Leonard. *"Box, Quotations from Chariman Mao."* WCBS-TV 2, 30 Sept. 1968. Reprinted in *NYTCR*, 1968, p. 231.

   Box is "indecipherable" and void of "visual values." Both plays are "pessimistic." "The decline of the West" is the theme of *Mao*. Performances are commendable.

277. Hazard, Forrest E. "The Major Theme in *Who's Afraid of Virginia Woolf?*" *CEA* 31 (Dec. 1968): 10-11.

Martha represents "the physical universe." George represents "the civilizing force of rational intelligence" determined to master and create union in civilization. George and Martha's successors--Nick and Honey--are symbols of the future generation who depart with this knowledge and will hopefully learn from it.

278. Jefferys, Allan. *"Box-Mao-Box."* WABC-TV 7, 30 Sept. 1968. Reprinted in *NYTCR,* 1968, p. 231.

    BM "is commanding theatre, brilliantly staged." Nancy Kelly and William Pendleton are "marvelous" and "fearfully real." The play makes one think as good theater should.

279. Kerensky, Oleg. "An Anti-Bayreuth *Tristan* by Menotti." *LT,* 10 July 1968, p. 8.

    BM at the Spoleto Festival "would seem to be about human selfishness, and the sheer lack of connexion between people and their problems. It is curiously effective, and very much helped by Alan Schneider's inventive direction and the performances of Conrad Yama as Mao and Nancy Kelly as the Long-winded Lady."

280. Kerr, Walter. "Mao—But What Message?" *NYT,* 17 March 1968, sec. 2, p. 1.

    BM at the Buffalo Arena Theater is tedious. Interest is maintained through the Long-winded lady. Connecting the fragmental ideas is difficult.

281. ———. "Walter Kerr's Opinion." *NYT,* 13 Oct. 1968. Reprinted in *NYTCR,* 1968, pp. 213-214.

Albee accurately relays in the Broadway production of *BW* that "form has slipped on us." Action arises out of an inactive play through "one rattled, embattled mind in search of itself." Nancy Kelly's acting and Alan Schneider's direction are commendable.

282. Lee, Robert C. "Albee in Paris." *Drama Critique*, 11 (Winter 1968): 38-39.

283. Marshall, Thomas F. "Edward Albee and the Nowhere Generation." *Mexico Quarterly Review*, 3 (1968): 39-47.

Albee's characters in *AD, BS, VW,* and *TA* can be grouped into the Then, Now, and Nowhere: "three generations moving progressively from a meaningful dynamic use of moral power toward an infeebled morality; three generations moving from fulfillment within a set of real values toward a meaningless, emasculated, narcissistic society."

284. Meyer, Ruth. "Language, Truth, and Illusion in *Who's Afraid of Virginia Woolf?*" *ETJ*, 20 (March 1968): 60-69.

The characters use overly precise and cliché-ridden language and play false roles to mask pain. This avoidance of reality results in ambiguous language and a difficulty in distinguishing between truth and illusion.

285. Nelson, Benjamin. "Avant-Garde Dramatists from Ibsen to Ionesco." *Psychoanalytic Review* 55 (1968): 505-512.

Albee's style is briefly discussed on pp. 506-507. He is labeled "Freudian" because his study of family relationships resemble "group analytical sessions." The theme of "sexual perversions establish themselves as familiar elements of character, action, and dialogue" in his play.

286. Otten, Terry. "Ibsen and Albee's Spurious Children." *CD* 2 (Summer 1968): 89–93.

   VW and Ibsen's *Little Eyolf* are compared.

287. Probst, Leonard. *"Box-Mao-Box."* NBC-TV 4, 30 Sept. 1968. Reprinted in *NYTCR*, 1968, p. 231.

   "The Decline of the West," according to Albee, is due to noncommunication. The play has many "intellectual word games" and is "an adventure and a breakthrough to a new form."

288. Rutenberg, Michael. "Edward Albee: Playwright in Protest." *P,* Oct.-Nov. 1968, pp. 28-34.

   DB is concerned with "man's responsibility to man." Harry and Edna effectively act as catalysts to bring about this theme. Albee blames the father for the predicament rather than the mother. Tobias attempts to amend the past but change is impossible. The article is excerpted from Rutenberg's book (see no. 343, pp. 137-164).

289. Sandoe, James. *LJ,* 93 (Aug. 1968): 2895.

   A book review of *EG* finds the play lacking in Albee's usual "hot-debated symbolism" and any new ideas.

290. Simon, John. "Theatre Chronicle." *Hudson Review,* Winter 1968-1969, pp. 702-712.

   A review of the Broadway production of *BM* is offered on pp. 703-705. The play is a "fugue" lacking in dramatic development. It is "the same ambitious, artificial, circumlocutory prose Albee keeps elaborating in his later, sterile works."

291. Simpson, Herbert M. "*Tiny Alice:* Limited Affirmation in a Conflict Between Theatre and Drama." *Forum H,* 6 (Fall-Winter): 43-46.

Split focus of plot, character, and dramatic action makes *TA* confusing. The play attempts to play on too many dramatic levels, none of which lead to dramatic progression. The play also loses dramatic purpose through theatricalism.

292. Skloot, Robert. "The Failure of *Tiny Alice.*" *P,* Feb.-March 1968, pp. 79-81.

TA lacks "consistency in theme, in character, in action, in symbol, image or idea." Albee attempts "to say something consistently meaningful, rather than consciously saying everything obscurely."

293. Storrer, William Allan. "A Comparison of Edward Albee's *Who's Afraid of Virginia Woolf?* as Drama and as Film." Ph.D. dissertation, Ohio University, 1968. Abstracted in *DA,* 29 (1969): 3544-3545A.

The movie version offers more settings, places emphasis on Martha's tragedy rather than George's, and eliminates Albee's "Decline of the West" theme. The adaptation to screen "is a positive comment on the universality of Albee's dramatic expression and the flexibility of the cinema."

294. Styan, J.L. *The Dark Comedy,* pp. 214-217. 2d ed. London: Cambridge University Press, 1968.

Parallels between Albee and Williams' writing styles and characters are evident. Kilroy in *Camino Real* is akin to the Young Man in *AD* and *SB*, and George and Martha resemble Maggie and Brick in *Cat on a Hot Tin Rof*. *DB* "is written self-consciously Eliotese. . . . " His most successful play is *VW* which loses its comedy through the child symbol.

295. Sullivan, Dan. "Theater: Albee in Croatian." *NYT*, 4 July 1968, p. 13.

A Yugoslavian production of *VW* is "too European" and the ending suggests that Martha and George's marriage will be better.

296. ———. "Theater: Albee's *Bessie Smith* and *Dream* Revived." *NYT*, 3 Oct. 1968, p. 55.

BS resembles Williams and *AD* recalls Ionesco. Albee's voice, however, is unique. *AD* is a "minor American masterpiece." Cast and direction are commendable. The production was given by the Theater '69 Playwrights Repertory.

297. Vos, Nelvin. *Eugene Ionesco and Edward Albee: A Critical Essay*. Edited by Roderick Jellema. Grand Rapids: Eerdmans, 1968.

Albee and Ionesco's "dramatic motifs" are examined. Both men began with satire, moved to confrontation with the absurd, and finally "dramatized the tragic futility of living within the absurd, of living without hope." Parallels between the two men are drawn through analyses of *SB, AD, ZS, VW, TA,* and *DB*. A short biography of Albee is offered on pp. 45-46.

298. Watts, Richard. "Edward Albee's New Experiment." *NYP*, 1 Oct. 1968. Reprinted in *NYTCR*, 1968, p. 229.

BM is "self-indulgent" but "represents a steadily interesting experiment by a bold dramatic explorer." The cliché-ridden characters are effectively combined in a musical form. Cast, set, and direction are commendable.

299. Weales, Gerald. "Box Seat." *Cwealth*, 25 Oct. 1968, pp. 120-122.

"What Albee is up to [in *BM*] is not so much an examination of the contemporary situation as the rhetorical and artistic means of coping with it, an implicit critique on his own work that is harsher than that made by even his most vehement critics. . . . "

300. West, Anthony. "Theatre." *Vogue*, 15 Nov. 1968, p. 92.

Unlike Judith Malina and Julian Beck who prefer stage activity over language, Albee in *BM* makes "the stage action a minimal appendage to a mud slide of meaningless chatter."

301. Woods, Linda. "Isolation and the Barrier of Language in *The Zoo Story.*" *Research Studies*, 36 (Sept. 1968): 224-231.

Albee uses theme and language to express the inability to communicate in the twentieth century. Peter isolates himself through trite replies and Jerry's "flippancy" serves the same purpose. Their lack of communication is very communicative, however, to the audience.

1969

302. Bannon, Barbara A. *PW,* 24 Feb. 1969, p. 60.

The book review of *BM* describes it as "a contrapuntal play of meanings" and considers it fascinating reading fare. "Albee may be losing himself in a desert of meanings but he's unique, and buffs will want these plays."

303. Barnes, Clive. "The Stage: American Conservatory Presents Albee's *Tiny Alice*."*NYT*, 30 Sept. 1969. Reprinted in *NYTCR*, 1969, p. 254.

TA hasn't diminished after five years. The theme is "the surprise and necessity of martyrdom." The production is "impeccable" with good interpretation by director William Ball.

304. Bigsby, C.W.E. *Albee*. Edinburgh: Oliver and Boyd, 1969.

Analyses of Albee's life and works before 1958, *ZS, AD, SB, BS, VW, SC, TA, DB,* and *M* are offered. The fusion of European absurdism into "American tradition," and his "acerbic wit" are his contributions to the American theater.

305. Brown, Daniel. "Albee's Targets." *Satire Newsletter*, Spring 1969, pp. 46-52.

Albee's satiric attacks in *ZS, DB, BS, VW, SB, AD, TA, M,* and *DB* on "the institutions of the middle class, motherhood, and marriage are undermined for their own sakes." Albee is "feared and excoriated" more than "praised" because his implicit norms for social behavior are anti-social.

306. Brustein, Robert. *The Third Theatre*, pp. 83-86. New York: Knopf, 1969.

Reprints of reviews of *M* and *DB* (1966), and *EG* (1967) first published in *NewR* are offered.

307. Bryson, Rhett B. Jr. "The Setting and Lighting Design for *The Ballad of the Sad Cafe.*" M.F.A. thesis, University of Georgia, 1969.

308. Chapman, John. "Revival of *Tiny Alice:* Still Metafuzzical Bore." *NYDN,* 30 Sept. 1969. Reprinted in *NYTCR,* 1969, p. 256.

"Except for its brilliant opening scene, . . . *Tiny Alice* remains a garrulous and quite tiresome metaphysical comedy-drama." The performances, however, are "good."

309. Clurman, Harold. "Theater." *N,* 27 Oct. 1969, p. 451.

William Ball's production of *TA* "is easier to take than the stodgy New York production of 1965." The sets "are efficient." Stage business and acting are deliberate: "The audience is not permitted to overlook a thing." This "well disciplined staginess" grows tiresome due to "shallow" theatrical devices. Thus, the play remains "Albee's weakest and most pretentious play."

310. Cohn, Ruby. *Currents in Contemporary Drama.* Bloomington: Indiana University Press, 1969.

A general treatment of Albee with emphasis on *VW, ZS, TA,* and *BM* is provided throughout. Albee has obtained his form from European playwrights, but his dialogue is unique. "Under a veneer of realism, Albee had been shifting his emphasis from America's social illusion to man's metaphysical illusion."

311. ———. *Edward Albee.* Pamphlets on American Writers, no. 77. Minneapolis: University of Minnesota Press 1969.

Annotated Bibliography 1968 – 1977

SB, AD, BS, TA, ZS, VW, TA, and DB are analyzed with emphasis on Albee's affinity with European absurdism. A brief biography, a selected bibliography of plays, essays, current American reprints, and critical studies from 1961-1967 are offered.

312. Cooke, Richard P. "The Theater: *Tiny Alice* at ANTA." *WSJ*, 1 Oct. 1969. Reprinted *NYTCR*, 1969, p. 255.

    The revival is fairly effective. The performances, lighting design, and setting design are notable. The play remains irritating but proves "Albee's talent for providing theatrical fascination."

313. Crinkley, Richmond. "The Loss of Privacy." *NR*, 30 Dec. 1969, p. 1334.

    The ACT production of *TA* is inventive but cannot compensate for the weak script. Albee dwells upon "spiritual crisis," an overworked subject. Julian is a product of the Sixties and his private dilemma is no longer interesting.

314. Dieb, Ronald Kenneth. "Patterns of Sacrifice in the Plays of Arthur Miller, Tennessee Williams, and Edward Albee." Ph.D. dissertation, University of Denver, 1969. Abstracted in *DA*, 30 (1970): 5104A.

    The effectiveness of Miller, Williams, and Albee's adaptation of sacrificial ritual patterns to modern terms is examined. Unlike his two contemporaries, Albee employs "sacrificial justification" which "fails to resolve his dramatic conflict realistically since he denies his characters the opportunity to undergo the change which should accompany the preparation for and the fulfillment of the act of sacrifice." *ZS*, *VW*, and *TA* are cited.

315. Dozier, Richard J. "Adultery and Disappointment in *Who's Afraid of Virginia Woolf?*" *MD*, 11 (Feb. 1969): 432-436.

The third act lacks dramatic integrity because George's sacrifice of the child over Martha's adultery constitutes a shift in game rules from the first two acts. Albee wished either to end the play optimistically or could not end the game satisfactorily.

316. Duncan, Nancy K. "Study, Analysis, and Discussion of Two Roles for Performance: Hecuba in *Trojan Women* and Julia in *A Delicate Balance*." M.F.A. thesis, University of Iowa, 1969.

317. English, Emma Jean Martin. "Edward Albee: Theory, Theme, Technique." Ph.D. dissertation, Florida State University. Abstracted in *DA*, 30 (1970): 5103A.

The study 1) formulates Albee's theory of drama through his play *FY* and his comments in interviews; 2) reveals Albee's theme "condition of man"; and 3) examines his skill at combining musical form with dramatic structure in *BM* and *VW*.

318. Fischer, Gretl Kraus. "Edward Albee and Virginia Woolf." *Dalhousie Review*, 49 (Summer 1969): 196-207.

Parallels in theme are drawn between *VW* and Virginia Woolf's short story "Lappin and Lapinova" and novel *To the Lighthouse*.

319. Force, William M. "The 'What' Story? or Who's Who at the Zoo?" *Studies in the Humanities*, 1 (Winter 69-70): 47-53. Reprinted in *Cos* 2 (1972): 71-82.

The study recounts the diverse interpretations of *ZS* by critics.

320. Gaines, Robert A. "The Truth and Illusion Conflict in the Plays of Edward Albee." M.A. thesis, University of Maryland, 1969.

321. Gill, Brendan. "The Theater." *NY*, 11 Oct. 1969, pp. 85-86.

    The American Conservatory Theater revival of *TA* "isn't in the true Albee vein at all." "Hysteria," sums up William Ball's direction and Julian's death scene "teeters on the brink of being extremely funny." Paul Shenar as Julian gives an uneven performance.

322. Gottfried, Martin. "Theatre." *WWD*, 30 Sept. 1969. Reprinted in *NYTCR*, 1969, p. 256.

    Though *TA* is "silly," it is "Albee's strongest and most original—and most theatrical play." Since his last production of *TA* two years ago in San Francisco, director William Ball has made the proceedings less theatrical and minimized homosexual interpretation. The production is "tame," the music "thin," the sets "skimpy," and the cast nice.

323. Guernsey, Otis L., ed. *BP of 1968-1969*. New York: Dodd, Mead, 1969.

    Production notes of Theater 1969 Playwrights Repertory productions of *BM*, *BS*, *AD*, and *ZS* (pp. 379-380) and Ateljie 212 production of *VW* (pp. 425-426) are offered.

324. Harris, Leonard. *"Tiny Alice."* WCBS-TV 2, 29 Sept. 1969. Reprinted in *NYTCR*, 1969, p. 257.

The revival by ACT is "weaker in key areas than the original" particularly in the roles of Brother Julian and Miss Alice. "Physical flair" and "splashy effects" do not solve this metaphysical mystery. The play concerns "man's birth, fall from innocence, and death."

325. Hewes, Henry. "The Theater." *SR,* 18 Oct. 1969, p. 20.

ACT's "intensely theatrical" production of *TA* "is magnificent and thrilling theater" which "recognizes the surreality of Albee's fantastic creation. . . . " Acting, setting, costumes, and lighting are commendable.

326. Jansky, Ann Leah Lauf. "Albee's First Decade: An Evaluation." Ph.D. dissertation, St. Louis University, 1969. Abstracted in *DA,* 30 (1970): 3462A.

Albee's technical playwriting skills and use of language are marred only by his "temptation to drive home a social or ethical point."

327. Kauffman, Stanley. "On Theater." *NewR,* 1 Nov. 1969, p. 22.

The script of *TA* "seems worse" after five years. The ACT revival employs an abundance of campy stage devices to maintain attention. Paul Shenar as Julian cannot sustain "a part that is an author's willful conceit," and DeAnn Mears as Miss Alice is "sexless . . . to the point of transvestitism."

328. Kerr, Walter. "An Improved *Alice,* A Flattened *Flea.*" *NYT,* 12 Oct. 1969. Reprinted in *NYTCR,* 1969, pp. 251–252.

The ACT production of *TA* is an improvement over the Broadway production, yet the script remains elusive. Harry Frazier as the Cardinal overacts, but

Mears as Miss Alice and Shenar as Julian are commendable.

329. ———. *Thirty Plays Hath November: Pain and Pleasure in the Contemporary Theater.* New York: Simon and Schuster, 1969.

Albee is mentioned throughout with emphasis on *VW, SC, M,* and *TA.* Overall, he "pursues schema rather than invention." Newspaper reviews of *TA* (1964) and *EG* (1967) are reprinted.

330. Kolin, Phillip C. "A Classified Edward Albee Checklist." *S,* 6 (Sept. 1969): 16–32.

Four hundred–forty bibliographical items on Albee from 1958–1968 featuring interviews, dissertations, works by Albee, articles and books on Albee, and foreign citations are offered. The work lists many newspaper reviews on Albee's works outside the New York area.

331. Kroll, Jack. "ACT in New York." *NW,* 13 Oct. 1969, p. 125.

The ACT production of *TA* is energetic but hollow due to Albee's script. Direction "signifies a nothing that perhaps was never there."

332. Lambert, J.W. "Plays in Performance." *QTR,* Spring 1969, pp. 117–119.

The Royal Shakespeare Company's production of *DB* as a whole is not satisfying. Some cast members, set design, and direction are questionable.

333. Lewis, Theophilus. *"Tiny Alice." AM*, 18 Oct. 1969, p. 342.

The ACT revival is "handsomely mounted." The symbolic meaning of the characters is discussed.

334. Lucey, William F. "Albee's *Tiny Alice:* Truth and Appearance." *Ren*, 21 (Winter 1969): 76–80.

Having abandoned the church, Julian seeks to lose his "illusion of innocence" and "approach truth" through Alice and the community. He uses his imagination when this route is impossible.

335. Mandanis, Alice. "Symbol and Substance in *Tiny Alice.*" *MD*, 12 (May 1969): 92–98.

TA is a symbolic modern tragedy and a "metaphysical dream play" based on an old theme: the sacrifice of the individual for the sake of the group.

336. Mussoff, L. "Medium Is the Absurd: Address November 1968." *English Journal*, 58 (April 1969): 566–570.

ZS is an "excellent opener to Absurdist plays" for high schoolers because it is easier to comprehend than plays by Beckett or Ionesco. Though "students always find it hysterically funny," they have more difficulty understanding *AD*.

337. Porter, Thomas E. "Fun and Games in Suburbia: *Who's Afraid of Virginia Woolf?*" In *Myth and Modern American Drama*, pp.225–247. Detroit: Wayne State University Press, 1969.

Albee stresses "the breakdown of real communion

between individuals." He satirically comments upon "the success myth, the image of American manhood and womanhood, the institution of marriage itself." The games, the ritual, and dramatic structure contain romantic mythical elements.

338. Post, Robert M. "Cognitive Dissonance in the Plays of Edward Albee." *QJS*, 55 (Feb. 1969): 54–60.

Albee's characters display cognitive dissonance—"that discrepancy that may occur between what a person believes and what he says or does"—through marital troubles, sex role reversals, and reality-illusion duality in *ZS*, *SB*, *AD*, *BS*, *VW*, *TA*, *DB*, and *EG*.

339. ———. "Fear Itself: Edward Albee's *A Delicate Balance*." *CLA*, 13 (Dec. 1969): 163–171.

"Fear, caused at once by the knowledge of the empty lives they lead and lack of knowledge about their actual beings, permeates the characterizations in *Delicate Balance*. The characters want love; they do not want to be alone; they want to replace displacement with belonging."

340. Probst, Leonard. *"Tiny Alice."* NBC–TV 4, 29 Sept. 1969. Reprinted in *NYTCR*, 1969, p. 257.

The ACT revival is more enjoyable because of "more romp and less pomp." Stressing theatricality over religious mystery makes the play less mysterious and funnier.

341. Rand, Calvin. "Albee's Musical *Box–Mao–Box*." *Hum*, Jan.–Feb. 1969, p. 27.

A review of the Broadway production finds its contrapuntal structure a "novelty." The play itself, however, is tedious, pretentious and reiterates old themes of "the discipline of the art and the chaos of life, the decline of the West, and power of the East, the toughness of the past and the flabbiness of today. . . ."

342. Roth, Emilou. "The Family Structure of Edward Albee's Plays." M.A. thesis, University of Kansas, 1969.

343. Rutenberg, Michael. *Edward Albee: Playwright in Protest.* New York: DBS, 1969. Reprinted New York: Avon, 1970.

Albee is "the single hope for an almost ossified Broadway theatre." A general analysis of *AD, BS, FY, BM, DB, SC, M, TA, ZS,* and *EG* with frequent reference to other critical opinions is offered. The last chapter features two interviews with Albee (see nos. 120 and 124). A chronological list of premieres up to *BM* is included.

344. Sanders, Walter Ernest. "The English-Speaking Game Drama: Beckett, Pinter, and Albee." Ph.D. dissertation, Northwestern University, 1969. Abstracted in *DA,* 30 (1970): 5001–5002A.

"Beckett, Pinter, and Albee are game dramatists in the sense of using games as the central principle of both the structure and theme of their plays." The game motifs in *VW* and *ZS* are analyzed following a discussion of twentieth century game dramatists and the formulation of a definition of "game."

345. Sandoe, James. *LJ,* 94 (July 1969): 2635.

A book review of *BM* finds the plays "incomprehensible" and "curious." They "arouse ineffective irritation and an awful temptation to call Mr. Albee insufferably cute."

346. Sellin, Eric. "Absurdity and the Modern Theatre." *CLA,* 12 (March 1969): 199–204.

Albee is not an absurdist in the vein of Beckett and Ionesco because his plays do not "deal with estrangement and character *isolation.*" Beckett and Ionesco's absurdism is discussed.

347. Shorter, Eric. "Plays in Performance: Regions." *QTR,* Autumn 1969, p. 36.

The Worcester Repertory Company's production of *SC* features a good cast, but scene changes and excessive narration hamper the effect of "a clumsy, yet fascinating play."

348. Steadman, Dan. "An Analysis of the Plot Technique Used in Three of Edward Albee's Plays." M.A. thesis, University of Nebraska, 1969.

349. "The Theater." *T,* 17 Oct. 1969, p. 72.

The ACT production of *"Tiny Alice* cannot really be revived since it was never alive. . . . The metaphysical blah about God, saintliness, and martyrdom are as obfuscating as ever."

350. *Tiny Alice* Is Branded Offensive in Singapore." *NYT* , 24 July 1969, p. 13.

The production, sponsored by the University of Singapore Society, was stopped "on the grounds that it might offend Roman Catholics."

351. Tucker, John Bartholomew. *"Tiny Alice."* WABC–TV 7, 29 Sept. 1969. Reprinted *NYTCR,* 1969, p. 257.

The ACT production of *TA* is "confusing," the company is "good, solid," and the play maintains interest "except for the third act. . . . "

352. Wardle, Irving. "London Sees the New Albee." *LT*, 15 Jan. 1969, p. 6.

Albee's prose in *DB* is excellent and his interweaving of themes is graceful. The play, however, never achieves universality. Peter Hall's direction of the Aldwych Theatre production is ineffective. Commendable performances are given by Michael Horndon, Peggy Ashcroft, and Patience Collier.

353. Watts, Richard. *NYP*, 30 Sept. 1969. Reprinted in *NYTCR*, 1969, p. 256.

TA remains "enigmatic," "irritating," and has grown "more bewildering." The ACT production, however, is handsome.

354. Weales, Gerald. "Edward Albee: Don't Make Waves." In *The Jumping-Off Place: American Drama in the 1960s*, pp. 24–53. New York: Macmillan, 1969.

This history of and general critical attitude toward *ZS*, *VW*, *TA*, and *DB* are recounted. "Separateness" and man's unsuccessful effort to make contact are recurring themes in his works. Language has steadily become more important than dramatic situation.

355. Willeford, William. "The Mouse in the Model." *MD*, 12 (Sept. 1969): 135–145.

Albee combines Christianity, Greek myth, and legend to affirm the necessity of mystery in confronting our sins. A discussion of Pauline Martin's article on *TA* in *Cwealth*, 16 Sept. 1966, is featured, also.

1970

356. Brown, Terence. "Harmonia Discord and Stochastic Process: Edward Albee's *A Delicate Balance.*" *Re: Arts and Letters,* 3 (Spring 1970): 54–60.

    Albee successfully combines elements of realistic and symbolic drama to create a modern tragedy.

357. Campbell, Mary Elizabeth. "The Tempters in Albee's *Tiny Alice.*" *MD,* 13 (May 1970): 22–33.

    TA is a morality play. The Butler, Miss Alice, and The Lawyer are allegorical figures for the World, the Flesh, and the Devil, respectively. Their mission is to tempt Mankind (Brother Julian).

358. Falk, Eugene H. "*No Exit* and *Who's Afraid of Virginia Woolf?* A Thematic Comparison." *Studies in Philology,* 67 (July 1970): 406–417.

    The stripping away of illusions and the reliance upon others for identity can be found in the situation and characters of both plays.

359. Guernsey, Otis L., ed. *BP of 1969–1970.* New York: Dodd, Mead, 1970.

    Production notes of American Conservatory Theater's revival of *TA* are offered on pp. 297–298.

360. Hefling, Joel. "*Who's Afraid of Virginia Woolf?:* A Scene Design Project." M.A. thesis, Kansas State Teachers College-Emporia, 1970.

361. Lambert, J.W. "Plays in Performance: London." *QTR,* Spring 1970, pp. 15–17.

The Royal Shakespeare Company production of *TA* is enigmatic. Despite some good performances, the play is boring.

362. Langdon, Harry N. "A Critical Study of *Tiny Alice* by Edward Albee Focussing on Commanding Image and Ritual Form." Ph.D. dissertation, University of Iowa, 1970. Abstracted in *DA,* 31 (1970): 3080–3081A.

    A study of *TA*'s symbols and ritual forms is more beneficial than conventional plot analysis.

363. Lee, A. Robert. "Illusion and Betrayal: Edward Albee's Theatre." *Studies: An Irish Quarterly Review,* 59 (Spring 1970): 53–67.

    "It is the cheating, the pattern of betrayal and illusion, which are so powerfully focused for us in his plays [*ZS, AD, BS, VW, TA,* and *DB*] that constitute perhaps his greatest achievement."

364. Levy, Valery B. "Violence as Drama: A Study of the Development of the Use of Violence on the American Stage." Ph.D. dissertation, Claremont Graduate School and University Center, 1970. Abstracted in *DA,* 31 (1971): 6618–6619A.

    Albee, O'Neill, and Williams use language as aggression. Their "dialogue of cruelty," reminiscent of 19th century Strindbergian domestic dramas, "has been the tradition of violence in the American theater. . . ."

365. Lewis, Allan. *American Plays and Playwrights of the Contemporary Theatre,* pp. 85–88. 2d rev. ed. New York: Crown, 1970.

    The 1965 edition is updated with a discussion of *TA,*

DB, EG, and *BM. TA* is "a modern mystery play" that questions faith. *DB* "is one of the weakest in construction. . . . it has too much talk and too little action." *EG,* which has an "explosive" first act but dull second act, deals with materialism. *BM* is an attempt at experimental form. Overall, other writers greatly influence Albee's work.

366. "London Puzzles Over *Tiny Alice.*" *NYT,* 17 Jan. 1970, p. 24.

    Excerpts from the *Daily Telegraph,* the *Guardian, LT, Daily Mail,* and *Daily Express* reveal that "London's theater critics were generally baffled and disappointed. . . ."

367. Quigley, Martin and Richard Gortner. *Films in America, 1929–1969.* New York: Golden, 1970.

    A brief recapitulation of the film *VW* and its "unique place in motion picture history" is offered.

368. Ruben, Paul A. "The Effect of Voluntary and Forced Theatre Attendance on Attitudes Toward the Play *Who's Afraid of Virginia Woolf?,* Theatre in General and New Forms of Drama." M.A. thesis, Bowling Green State University, 1970.

369. Schupbach, Deanna Justina. "Edward Albee's America." Ph.D. dissertation, University of Texas at Austin, 1970. Abstracted in *DA,* 32 (1972): 4022–4023A.

    Character types in *ZS, BS, SB, AD, VW,* and *TA* are grouped into three generations and "arranged to project the author's interpretation of a changing American scene. . . ." Albee's thematic concern with "the dominance of the acquisitive values in the future" is realized through analysis.

370. Shelton, Lewis Edward. "Alan Schneider's Direction of Four Plays by Edward Albee: A Study in Form." Ph.D. dissertation, University of Wisconsin-Madison, 1971. Abstracted in *DA,* 32 (1972): 4754A.

Theatrical forms used by Schneider in *VW* (plot), *AD* (character), *TA* (thought), and *DB* (structure) are employed to clarify Albee's view of reality.

371. Shuster, Alvin. "Reaction in Wrong Places Closes 3 Plays in Prague." *Y,* 3 Feb. 1970, p. 5.

DB closes due to "the present practice of Czechs of expressing their unhappiness over the Soviet occupation by finding significant political meanings in seemingly innocuous situations in plays and films."

372. Terrien, Samuel. "Demons Also Believe: Parodying the Eucharist." *Christian Century,* 9 Dec. 1970, pp. 1481–1483.

Albee's blasphemous use of Christian ritual in *VW* is a constructive revolt against corrupt society and religious institutions and an affirmation of "man's unconscious need to expiate personal or collective guilt, to promote standards of communal responsibility, and thus to participate in man's being in the life of the universe and in the intelligent purpose of history. . . ."

373. "Voices from the Cube." *TLS,* 25 June 1970, p. 687.

A book review of *BM* finds a "sense of loss" theme common to both plays. *Box* borders on a "prose poem" and is Albee's most abstract piece. *Mao* is more realistic and "despite its quirky self-indulgence, the writing attains a very high level. . . ."

374. Von Szeliski, John. "Albee: A Rare *Balance.*" *TCL,* 16 (April 1970): 123–130.

   An analysis of "the style and content of the play's meanings" concludes that *DB* is "the best expression of the peculiar loneliness of our time which we have had in years, standing out in an age which desperately parades sensation and exhibition in the guise of 'drama.'"

375. Umberger, Norman C. "Edward Albee: The Development of Two Characters." M.A. thesis, West Virginia University, 1970.

376. Wardle, Irving. "Albee Presents a Poser." *LT,* 16 Jan. 1970, p. 13.

   Albee's style in *TA* is "baroque" because "he is less an innovator than a decorator of existing idioms." The play is influenced by Beckett, Durrenmatt, Genet, and Pinter. The theme is banal: "the 'Wonders of the World' represent the temptation to worship only what can be seen (hence Material culture); and that when Julian succumbs to it, he is lost. . . ." The Aldwych Theatre production is directed and performed commendably.

377. White, James E. "An Early Play by Edward Albee." *TCL,* 42 (March 1970): 98–99.

   Albee's early play, *Schism,* written when he was a senior in prep school, is a precursor to themes in *TA* and the grandmother figure in *SB* and *AD*. The play, however, has little merit.

378. Witherington, Paul. "Albee's Gothic: The Resonances of Cliché." *CD*, 4 (Fall 1970): 151–165.

   Albee employs the Gothic techniques of reduction, inversion, and recognition in his plays. Excluding his adaptations, all his plays are discussed. Emphasis is placed on *AD*, *VW*, *TA*, and *DB*.

1971

379. "*Ballad of the Sad Cafe.*" *LT*, 10 March 1971, p. 11.

   SC "is a curiously disappointing work." The narrator, reminiscent of the Stage Manager in *Our Town*, is excessive. The Leonard White production at the Thorndike Leatherhead Theatre is well done, however.

380. Barnes, Clive. "*All Over.*" *LT*, 30 March 1971, p. 10. Reprinted in *NYT*, 29 March 1971 and *NYTCR*, 1971, p. 322.

   AO "is a lovely, poignant, and deeply felt play" in which "the atmosphere of people rather than people themselves" predominates. The Broadway production has good direction, setting, and cast. For eight letters to the editor on this review, see "Albee—Again Controversy," *NYT*, 18 April 1971, sec. 2, p. 7.

381. Blades, Larry Thomas. "Williams, Miller, and Albee: A Comparative Study." Ph.D. dissertation, St. Louis University, 1971. Abstracted in *DA*, 32 (1972): 4600A.

The study examines the thematic relationship of the three authors in the areas of Society (ZS, *Battle of Angels, Death of a Salesman*), The Individual *(VW, A Streetcar Named Desire, The Misfits),* Guilt and Atonement *(TA, Black Masseur, After the Fall),* Sex and Marriage *(AD, Summer and Smoke, The Price),* and The Family *(DB, Glass Menagerie, View from the Bridge).*

382. Clurman, Harold. "Theater." *N*, 12 April 1971, pp. 476–477.

   AO "is the best play of several seasons. . . ." The stylistic and ritualistic Broadway production is "remarkably fine" and director Gielgud "has given Albee his most thoroughly realized interpretation." Conventional action becomes secondary to revelation of the characters. Through the theme of death, "Albee is saying that, despite all the hasty bickering, the fierce hostility and the mutual misunderstandings which separate us, we need each other."

383. ———. "Theater." *N*, 3 May 1971, pp. 570–571.

   Albee "expresses a genuine response to the aridity of much that we now sense about us. . . there is an emotional significance in his writing that I find moving." The Broadway production could have "more body" in characterization and be played in a more intimate theater.

384. Cohn, Ruby. "Albee's Box and Ours." *MD*, 14 (Sept. 1971): 137–141.

   Albee's statement on art form in *BM* supersedes his theme of human mortality. His characters, "skillfully played instrument[s]," reveal that only art can bring about change and death is unalterable.

385. ———. "The Verbal Murders of Edward Albee," pp. 130–169. In *Dialogue in American Drama*. Bloomington: Indiana University Press, 1971.

A revision of previous criticism on Albee up to *DB* (see no. 311) with additional comments on *EG* and *BM* offered.

386. Crinkley, Richmond. "The Development of Edward Albee." *NR*, 1 June 1971, pp. 602–604.

"Hypersensitivity makes *All Over*. . . a beautiful and exciting piece of theater. . . . Albee's most satisfying achievement" since *DB*. The lack of action is akin to Pinter and Beckett. Albee, however, would have more faith in his work and avoid responding to negative criticism. "The production at the Martin Beck [Broadway] is fine, polished to a nice, false sheen."

387. Delatte, Anne Perkins. "Alienation, Illusion, and Confrontation: A Study of Edward Albee's Statement of the Condition of Man," [*ZS, SB, AD, VW, TA, DB*, and *BM*.] M.A. thesis, University of New Orleans, 1971.

388. Dannenberg, William J. "A Production of *The Ballad of the Sad Cafe*, by Edward Albee." M.F.A. thesis, University of North Carolina—Greensboro, 1971.

389. Engle, William Francis. "Truth Versus Illusion and Sterility in the Writings of Edward Albee: A Study of Four Plays." M.A. thesis, California State College at Fullerton, 1971. Abstracted in *MA*, 9 (1971): 239.

"Throughout his plays, Albee emphasizes man's need to live with truth. . . man will only be satisfied with truth not false illusions." *ZS, AD, VW,* and *TA* deal with two "submotifs" on the "truth vs. illusion" theme: "man's inability to communicate and the subsequent sterility."

390. Frankel, Haskel. "*All Over* Is Mr. Albee's Best Play, Masking Love in Hostility." *NO*, 29 March 1971, p. 21.

Albee analyzes love with "control and refinement" instead of violence. The Broadway cast is "more than excellent," particularly Colleen Dewhurst and Jessica Tandy.

391. Gill, Brendan. "The Theater." *NY*, 3 April 1971, p. 95.

AO "is resourcefully plotted, and is written with skill in care, in a heightened language" but lacks "all the means by which we might have been encouraged to care about his assortment of troubled souls." The Broadway cast is "exemplary" and the set "handsome."

392. Gilman, Richard. *Common and Uncommon Masks: Writings on Theatre, 1961–1970,* pp. 133–136. New York: Random House, 1971.

Reviews on *VW (Cwealth*, 9 Nov. 1962) and *TA (NW,* 11 Jan. 1965) are reprinted.

393. Gottfried, Martin. "Theater." *WWD*, 29 March 1971. Reprinted in *NYTCR*. 1971, p. 322.

Albee's return to "surrealism" is "boring." The "characters never converse or behave or interact or exist." The "simple-minded" script offered director Gielgud no creativity. The actors are "fine but bewildered." Albee's "inability to feel for other people" colors his artistry and makes *AO* worthless.

394. Guernsey, Otis L., ed. *BP of 1970–1971*. New York: Dodd, Mead, 1971.

Broadway production notes on *AO*, regional production notes of Albee plays, and production statistics on his plays are offered throughout.

395. Harris, Leonard. "*All Over.*" WCBS–TV 2, 28 March 1971. Reprinted in *NYTCR*, 1971, p. 323.

Albee's accustomed "wit," "wordplay," and "epigrams" are absent. The Broadway cast is "excellent," but the drama remains Albee's "least satisfying."

396. Hayman, Ronald. *Edward Albee.* London: Heinemann, 1971.

A chapter of criticism and analysis is devoted to *ZS, BS, SB, AD, VW, SC, TA, M, DB, EG,* and *AO,* respectively. Albee's plays reflect Ionesco's influence, yet offer more social criticism. A biographical outline 1928–1970 and a selected bibliography, 1962–1970 are included.

397. Hewes, Henry. "The Theater." *SR,* 10 April 1971, p. 54.

Albee criticizes in *AO* "indecisiveness" and "examines the myth upon which the meaningfulness of marriage and love is based." Flatness of some of the characters is the major disappointment in the Broadway production. Gielgud's direction is apparently faithful to the playwright's vision. The setting is not distracting yet "fails to supply a feeling of warmth and of being in a house where old tradition is passing." Jessica Tandy, Colleen Dewhurst, and Betty Field are notable in their roles.

398. Higgins, David M. "Existential Valuation in Five Contemporary Plays: Miller, Pinter, Beckett, Albee, Genet," M.A. thesis, Bowling Green State University, 1971.

399. Hinds, Carolyn M. "Albee's *The American Dream*." *Ex*, 30 (Oct. 1971): Item 17.

    James Thomson's 1865 definition of the word "bumble" explains Albee's use of the word in *AD:* "a child neither free or alive morally and intellectually but emasculated, prefabricated by superficial standards of Middle Class America."

400. Houghton, Norris. *The Exploding Stage: An Introduction to Twentieth Century Drama*, pp. 186–198 *et passim*. New York: Weybright and Talley, 1971.

    ZS, AD, SB, VW, TA, AD, DB, and *BM* are analyzed with frequent reference to other interpretations, particularly Michael E. Rutenberg's *Edward Albee: Playwright in Protest* (see no. 343).

401. Hughes, Catherine. "Albee's Deathwatch." *AM*, 5 June 1971, pp. 593–595. Reprinted in *PP*, June 1971, p. 30.

    AO is artificial in language and has very little to say about living or dying. The Broadway production reiterates Albee's failure to become O'Neal's successor.

402. Kalen, T.E. "Club Bore." *T*, 5 April 1971, p. 69. Reprinted in *NYTCR*, 1971, p. 320.

    The Broadway production of *AO* is "deadly dull." The play's "grand themes" lack "any dramatic urgency or compelling emotional life." The sterotypical characters are "thin and sketchy."

403. Kauffman, Stanley. "On Theater." *NewR,* 17 April 1971, p. 24.

Albee attempts to impress the audience with his intelligence through elevated language in *AO*. The names of the characters and the "heavily symbolic set" give the play allegorical status. Unlike allegory, however, it lacks a central theme. Gielgud directs in stage pictures and the cast suffers with the exception of Neil Fitzgerald.

404. Kerr, Walter. "Albee's *All Over*—The Living Are Dead, Too." *NYT,* 4 April 1971, sec. 2, p. 1.

Like *BM, AO* remains "remote, detached, noncommittal." The setting regrettably underscores the feeling.

The cast is a perfect ensemble, but the characters are lifeless dramatically. The dialogue is "self-conscious, languidly 'literary,' knotty, and sometimes unmanageable for stage purposes." John Gielgud staged his actors "plausibly."

405. Kilkner, M.J. "Children and Childishness in the Plays of Edward Albee." *P,* Aug.–Sept. 1971, pp. 252–256.

ZS, SB, AD, and *VW* are analyzed for their childish elements (games, actions, names). Albee finds childhood natural but negates childishness. His "central characters seem never quite able to escape childhood in some form or another at least not without living through a crisis." *DB, TA, BM,* and *BS* are mentioned briefly.

406. Kroll, Jack. "The Disconnection." *NW*, 5 April 1971, p. 52. Reprinted in *NYTCR*, 1971, p. 321.

AO "is a depressing event in an enigmatic career." The characters lack life and the set "is portentous and melodramatic." The "deadness" of the piece lies chiefly in the language. Dewhurst and Tandy are the Broadway production's assets.

407. Lambert, J.W. "Plays in Performance: London." *QTR*, Summer 1971, p. 37.

The Thorndike Theatre Leatherhead production of *SC* lacks an effective script and a real dwarf.

408. Leyden, William Henry. "Social Protest and the Absurd: A Reading of the Plays of Edward Albee." Ph.D. dissertation, University of Oregon, 1971. Abstracted in *DA*, 32 (1972): 6434A.

Albee's writing style is a blend of social protest and Absurdist tradition. An examination of traditional absurdism and protest plays of the twentieth century reveal *ZS* and *BS* as "primarily social protest dramas'; *SB*, *AD*, *VW*, *DB*, *M*, *EG*, and *BM* as a mixture of social protest and Absurdism; and *TA* as pure absurdism.

409. Melloan, George. "The Theater." *WSJ*, 30 March 1971. Reprinted in *NYTCR*, 1971, pp. 321–322.

AO may not be as powerful as *VW*, but it "is a great deal better than most of what modern dramatists can offer." The play is interesting because of Albee's "prose, the seriocomic interplay of characters, and at times profound treatment of its central subject, the psychology of the still-living in the presence of the soon-to-die."

410. Murray, Michael. "Albee's End Game." *Cwealth*, 3 April 1971, pp. 166–167.

Despite a good cast, the Broadway production of *AO* is hampered by lack of character distinctions and "elaborately precious" dialogue.

411. Myers, Charles Robert. "Games Structure in Selected Plays." Ph.D. dissertation, University of Iowa, 1971. Abstracted in *DA*, 32 (1971): 1676–1677A.

ZS, Shaw's *Doctor's Dilemma*, Congreve's *Way of the World*, and Shakespeare's *Othello* are structurally similar when applied to a hypothetical "game-structure" formula.

412. Myers, Joseph T. "A Comparison of the Two Leading Female Characters in Henrik Ibsen's *Hedda Gabler* and Edward Albee's *Who's Afraid of Virginia Woolf?*" M.A. thesis, University of Mississippi, 1971.

413. Newman, Edwin. *"All Over."* NBC-TV 4, 28 March 1971. Reprinted in *NYTCR*, 1971, p. 324.

The Broadway production is "windy and pretentious." The cast is commendable, "but John Gielgud's direction, joined to the play, suggests a parody of well-bred English drawing room drama."

414. Norton, Rictor Carl. "Folklore and Myth in *Who's Afraid of Virginia Woolf?*" *Ren*, 23 (Spring 1971): 159–167. Reprinted in "Studies of the Union of Love and Death. I. Heracles and Hylas: The Homosexual Archetype. II. The Pursuit of Ganymede. III. Folklore and Myth in *Who's Afraid of Virginia Woolf?* IV. *The Turn of the Screw:* Coincidental Oppositorum." Ph.D. disser-

tation, Florida State University, 1972. Abstracted in *DA,* 33 (1972): 5190–5191A.

The title, setting, animal and geographical allusions, and characters are analyzed for their mythical derivatives.

415. Novick, Julius. "The Distinguished Decadence of Edward Albee." *Hum,* July-Aug. 1971, pp. 34–35.

    The Broadway production of *AO* is well-mounted and resembles Eliot's drawing room pieces. Albee's "cold, remote, bloodless sytle," however, lacks substance.

416. Pease, Donald. *"Tiny Alice* (Edward Albee)" [phonotape]. Deland, Fla.: Everett/Edwards, 1971.

417. Ramsey, Roger. "Jerry's Northerly Madness." *NCL,* 1 (1971): 7–8.

    Hamlet and *ZS* are similar in their themes of "sullied flesh, indecision, poison, suicide," and particularly "madness."

418. Richardson, James G. "Division of Groundwork: Edward Albee's Adaptation of Carson McCullers' *The Ballad of the Sad Cafe."* M.A. thesis, University of Florida, 1971.

419. Richmond, Hugh M. "Shakespeare and Modern Sexuality: Albee's *Virginia Woolf* and *Much Ado."* In *Shakespeare's Sexual Comedy,* pp. 177–199. Indianapolis: Bobbs-Merrill, 1971.

    "Albee's *Virginia Woolf* shows that Shakespeare's conception of sexuality can be plausibly transposed into modern terms. . . ." George and Martha use verbal battles similar to Benedict and Beatrice's for expressing love and sympathy, demonstrating wit, and attaining wisdom. Albee also uses younger foils (Nick and Honey) and "Shakespeare's technique of therapeutic displacement."

420. Rissover, Frederic. "Beat Poetry, *The American Dream*, and the Alienation Effect." *Speech Teacher*, Jan. 1971, pp. 36–43.

Beat poetry of the late 1950s was interspersed throughout a production of *AD*. The poetry acted as a commentary on Albee's ideas and produced an alienating (Brechtian) effect. Excerpts from the script and a set floor plan are provided.

421. Rudin, Seymour. "Theatre Chronicle: Winter-Spring 1971." *Massachusetts Review*, 12 (Autumn 1971): 821–833.

Unlike *BM*, *AO*'s meaning . . . stubbornly refuses to emerge." The play illuminates Albee's literary decline and the "wasted" efforts of director and cast. The Broadway production is reviewed on p. 824.

422. Rudisell, Cecil Wayne. "An Analysis of the Martyr as a Dramatic Character in Three Plays by Edward Albee: *Tiny Alice, The Zoo Story*, and *A Delicate Balance*." M.A. thesis, American University, 1971. Abstracted in *MA*, 10 (1972): 285.

"The study analyzes, using historical examples, the concept of martyrdom by translating the religious experience into scientific psychological language. . . ."

423. Schubeck, John. *"All Over."* WABC-TV 7, 28 March 1971. Reprinted in *NYTCR*, 1971, p. 324.

Albee's "best" play has an "outstanding" cast. The play lacks dramatic builds which result in a "concert of words devoid of heavy emotional crescendos."

424. Sheed, Wilfred. *The Morning After: Selected Essays and Reviews*, pp. 165–167. New York: Farrar, Straus, and Giroux, 1971.

    The *DB* review "Liquor Is Thicker," *Cwealth*, 14 Oct. 1966, pp. 55–56, is reprinted.

425. Syna, Sy. "The Old Prof Takes the Stage." *P*, Feb.–March 1971.

    "These two plays [*VW* and Leroi Jones' *The Slave*,] widely divergent in approach, contain strange similarities: Each is set in the home of a college professor and a faculty; . . . and, more significantly, each contains a devastating portrait of the college professor. . . ." Both authors imply that "society was built on humanistic principles" and that "humanists have not been productive in the university setting."

426. Tolpegin, Dorothy D. "The Two Petaled Flower: A Commentary on Edward Albee's Play, *Tiny Alice*." *Cim R*, 14 (Jan. 1971): 17–30.

    "The play seems to carry out in setting, action, and characters the concept of twinned halves in which the images that materialize in one half, while not precisely duplicating those of the other, *do* reflect and reverberate in the other."

427. Wagner, Marlene Strome. "The Game-Play in Twentieth Century Absurdist Drama: Studies in Dramatic Technique." Ph.D. dissertation, University of Southern California, 1971. Abstracted in *DA*, 32 (1972): 4637A.

Game-playing in Albee, Beckett, Genet, and Pinter are analyzed in light of Richard Schechner's "Approaches to Criticism" (*TDR*, 1966, pp. 20–53) and Eric Berne's *Games People Play*. The games in *VW* "are a device to reveal the plot rather than a strict substitute for it."

428. Watt, Douglas. Albee's *All Over* Is Glacial Drama About a Death Watch." *NYDN*, 29 March 1971. Reprinted in *NYTCR*, 1971, p. 323.

AO is a "soap opera" which offers little suspense. The "lofty" language is difficult to follow and has little to say. Acting, directing, and setting are commendable.

429. Watts, Richard. "Theater." *NYP*, 29 March 1971. Reprinted in *NYTCR*, 1971, p. 320.

AO doesn't advance Albee's career. More information on the dying man is needed. Albee's prose style is good though it occasionally "takes on the suggestion of being the written word rather than actual speech. . . ." Acting is hampered by the writing.

430. Wellwarth, George. *The Theatre of Protest and Paradox*, pp. 321–336 *et passim*. 2d rev. ed. New York: New York University Press, 1971.

A reprint of *AD* and *ZS* criticism in "Hope Deferred: The New American Drama. Reflections on Edward Albee, Jack Richardson, Jack Gelber, and Arthur Kopit," *Literary Review* 7 (Autumn 1963): 8–15, are offered with added comments on *TA, DB,* and *BM*. *TA* is "meaningless" and akin to *Camino Real; DB* is an unsuccessful attempt at combining realism with absurdism; and *BM* is imitative of Beckett and an overly obvious political allegory which "remains incomprehensible on its own terms and undramatic. ..."

431. Westerfield, William. "A Production and Thesis of Edward Albee's *Everything in the Garden.*" M.A. thesis, University of Maryland, 1971.

432. Wilderman, Marie R. "The Ritual of Games in Three of Albee's Plays: *Who's Afraid of Virginia Woolf?*, *Tiny Alice,* and *The American Dream."* M.A. thesis, University of New Orleans, 1971.

433. Wimble, Barton. *LJ,* 96 (15 Sept. 1971): 2786.

The book review of *AO* states that lack of dramatic tension and color in the play "shows a masterful grammarian at work, a man totally remote from everyday life and humanity, one who has mined out his little vein of cold vindictiveness and must either learn humanity again or perish as an artist."

434. Winchell, Cedric R. "An Analysis of the Symbology in the Earlier Plays by Edward Albee." Ph.D. dissertation, University of California, Los Angeles, 1971. Abstracted in *DA,* 32 (1972): 6600A.

The "structural foundation of ego-development focusing on the crystalization of ego-consciousness of man from his pre-dawn state as elucidated by C.G. Jung and Erich Neumann . . . particularly the concept of individualization and controversion as expressed through symbology is used throughout the text to illustrate Albee's psychic development" in *ZS, FY, SB, AD,* and *BS.*

435. Agnihotri, S.M. "Child-Symbol and Imagery in Ed-

ward Albee's *Who's Afraid of Virginia Woolf?" Panjab University Research Bulletin* (Arts), 3 (Oct. 1972): 108–111.

VW is not escapist fare as Richard Schechner claims in "Who's Afraid of Edward Albee?" *Tulane Drama Review,* 7 (Spring 1963): 7–13. Through characters and imagery, Albee is making a serious statement on the tragic myth of a sterile civilization.

436. Argenio, Joseph. "Tobias: A Delicate Balance." M.F.A. thesis, Smith College, 1972.

437. Bachman, Charles R. "Albee's *A Delicate Balance:* Parable as Nightmare." *Revue des langues vivantes,* 38 (1972): 619–630.

Albee used *The Book of Tobit* to create "an ironic parable of modern man." *The Book* influenced the "central theme and structure of the drama."

438. Byars, John A. *Taming of the Shrew* and *Who's Afraid of Virginia Woolf?" Cim R,* 21 (Oct. 1972): 41–48.

In *VW,* "Albee's variation of the myth of woman as heroic test takes the familiar form it embodied in medieval literature, the taming of the shrew." The theme is "the struggle for dominance in marriage" as George the hero tames Martha the modern shrew through "suffering and symbolic destruction."

439. Cavan, Romilly. "Scripts." *PP,* July 1972, p. 81.

TA "possibly reads better than it plays." The text "bears all the distinctive hallmarks of his master-craftsmanship."

440. ———. "Scripts." *PP,* Aug. 1972, p. 64.

"For all its extreme self-consciousness *All Over* is both impressive and moving to read."

441. Doerry, Karl W. "Edward Albee's Modern Morality Plays." Ph.D. dissertation, University of Oregon, 1972. Abstracted in *DA*, 33 (1972): 2368–2369A.

    The study treats *ZS*, *VW*, *TA*, and *DB* as modern mystery and morality plays.

442. Duplessis, Rachel Blau. "In the Bosom of the Family: Evasions in Edward Albee." *Recherches anglaises et américaines*, 5 (1972): 85–96.

    Albee uses evasion in *VW*, *DB*, and *AD* to resolve contradictions posed at the end of the plays. He assumes that the solution lies in "assimilating all problems to family relationships, and curing them by reestablishing sexual stereotypes and killing (mutilating) the rival," or having problem characters exit from the play.

443. Fleming, William P., Jr. "Tragedy in American Drama: The Tragic Views of Eugene O'Neill, Tennessee Williams, Arthur Miller, and Edward Albee." Ph.D. dissertation, University of Toledo, 1972. Abstracted in *DA*, 33 (1972): 308A.

    The study offers characteristics of American tragedy as reflected in the four authors. "Man's search for reality" is Albee's major contribution to the seven distinctively American traits cited.

444. Guernsey, Otis L., ed. *BP of 1971–1972*. New York: Dodd, Mead, 1972.

    Notes and statistics on Albee's plays produced in regional theaters are listed throughout.

445. Gussow, Mel. "Theater: Albee's *Alice.*" *NYT,* 17 April 1972, p. 46.

   The Hartford Stage Company production is more satisfying than either the Broadway or ACT productions chiefly because of its simple staging. "The strength of this *Tiny Alice* is in the actors."

446. Hall, Roger Allan. "Edward Albee and His Mystery: A Structural and Thematic Analysis of *Who's Afraid of Virginia Woolf?* and *A Delicate Balance.*" M.A. thesis, Ohio State University, 1972.

447. Lambert, J.W. "Plays in Performance." London: *QTR,* Spring 1972, pp. 21–22.

   The slow pace of the Royal Shakespeare production of *AO* is only relieved by dialogue between The Mistress and The Wife.

448. Levene, Victoria E. "The House of Albee: A Study of the Plays of Edward Albee." Ph.D. dissertation, State University of New York at Binghamton, 1972. Abstracted in *DA,* 33 (1972): 317A.

   The progression of Albee's dramatic treatment of mother, father, and child figures in *ZS, AD, VW, TA, BS, DB,* and *AO,* his use of absurdist techniques and other playwrights' dramatic devices, and his "unique adaptation of musical composition to dialogue and play structure" are examined.

449. Lumley, Frederick. *New Trends in Twentieth Century Drama: A Survey Since Ibsen and Shaw,* pp. 319–324. 4th rev. ed. New York: Oxford University Press, 1972.

Themes of misogyny and American corruption pervade Albee's works. His strength is stylization which closely resembles Theatre of the Absurd. Albee's potential is great; he lacks, however, universality and coherence. *ZS, BS, AD, VW,* and *TA* are discussed.

450. Moore, Don D. "Albee's *The American Dream." Ex,* 30 (Jan. 1972): Item 44.

Grandma in *AD* and Lear's Fool in *King Lear* both speak the truth but are urged to go to bed.

451. Paolucci, Anne. *From Tension to Tonic: The Plays of Edward Albee.* Carbondale: Southern Illinois University Press, 1972.

Albee is "the only playwright after O'Neill who shows real growth, the only one who has made a serious effort to break away from the 'message' plays which have plagued our theater since O'Neill." Albee's view of life remains existential throughout the various forms of his dramas. *BS, ZS, SB, AD, VW, DB, AO,* and *BM* are analyzed and a selective bibliography is included.

452. Stark, John. "Camping Out: *Tiny Alice* and Susan Sontag." *P,* April–May, 1972, pp. 166–169.

The critical theories of Susan Sontag shed light on the play. Specifically, "both Albee and Miss Sontag are interested in a camp sensibility and the nature of art."

453. Steiner, Donald Lee. "August Strindberg and Edward Albee: The Dance of Death." Ph.D. dissertation, University of Utah, 1972. Abstracted in *DA,* 33 (1972): 766A.

Strindberg and Albee's dance of death "suggests the death of old patterns of thought and the rebirth of the mind as it enters a higher degree of awareness." Parallels are drawn between *VW* and *Dance of Death*, *ZS* and *Pariah,* and *TA* and *Ghost Sonata.*

454. Stephens, Suzanne Schaddelee. "The Dual Influence of the Plays of Edward Albee and the Specific Dramatic Forms and Themes Which Influenced Them." Ph.D. dissertation, Miami University, 1972. Abstracted in *DA*, 34 (1973): 342A.

    Albee's works constitute a fusion of American realistic-expressionistic drama and European absurdism. The purpose of the study "is to examine the work of Edward Albee in light of the dramatic influences that inform his labors and thereafter to analyze in each play the appropriateness of the relationship between its theme and the form which gives it substance."

455. Thompson, Howard. "Theater: *Virginia Woolf en Espanol.*" *NYT,* 15 Oct. 1972, p. 71.

    The Spanish Theater Repertory Company's offering is "an exceedingly fine production. . . . The play is so good it requires only pitch and orchestration."

456. Wardle, Irving. "An Albee Elegy." *LT,* 1 Feb. 1972, p. 10.

    AO says little and has cloudy symbolism. Albee "is growing increasingly fanatical about language." He expresses "suppressed antagonism" well, however. "Peter Hall's production does all that it can with the piece."

1973

457. Adler, Thomas P. "Albee's *Who's Afraid of Virginia Woolf?:* A Long Night's Journey into Day." *ETJ,* 25 (March 1973): 66–70.

    The child is sacrificed in an attempt to re-establish the marital balance between George and Martha and Nick and Honey.

458. Amacher, Richard E. and Margaret Rule, comps. *Edward Albee at Home and Abroad: A Bibliography.* New York: AMS, 1973.

    The work offers a "reasonably complete" collection of approximately one thousand primary and secondary sources in England, America, and foreign-speaking countries particularly Germany. The bibliography extends from 1958 to June 1968. Some subjective annotations are given.

459. Carr, Duane R. "St. George and the Snapdragons: The Influence of Unamuno on *Who's Afraid of Virginia Woolf?" AQ,* 29 (Spring 1973): 5–13.

    VW is akin to Miguel de Unamuno's existential philosophy of creating illusions to avoid nothingness. Unamuno's story "Saint Emmanuel, the Good, Martyr" and *VW* are compared.

460. Corrigan, Robert W. "Engagement/Disengagement in the Contemporary Theatre," pp. 278–282. In *The Theatre in Search of a Fix.* New York: Delacorte, 1973.

    A general analysis of *VW* describes it as "one of the best examples of the American theater's new maturity...." Albee's "truth and illusion" theme, the child symbol, and the games are sound devices. The ending suggests redemption.

461. Dollard, John. "The Hidden Meaning of *Who's Afraid...?" Connecticut Review,* 7 (Oct. 1973): 24–48.

    Passages of dialogue are analyzed for their possible thematic content and "to identify the hidden motives and conflicts, to decode the urgent action of the play."

462. Elsom, John. *Erotic Theatre,* pp. 220–227 *et passim.* London: Secker and Warburg, 1973.

    Albee and Pinter "are our new society dramatists" because they "manage to combine intellectual prestige with popularity" and "share the Edwardian preoccupation with good dialogue." Albee's family relationships in *VW* and *DB* are similar to Williams. Both plays are vague and amateurishly analyze family relationships.

463. Falb, Lewis. *American Drama in Paris, 1945–1970: A Study of Critical Reception,* pp. 69–76. Chapel Hill: University of North Carolina Press, 1973.

    Overall, the public enjoyed Albee's work more than critics. *VW, AD,* and *ZS* were not relevant to Parisians and had "fundamental weaknesses in psychology." *DB* was disappointing to audience and critics.

464. Guernsey, Otis L., ed. *BP of 1972–1973.* New York: Dodd, Mead, 1973.

    Notes and statistics on Albee's plays produced in regional theaters are listed throughout.

465. Holtan, Orley I. *"Who's Afraid of Virginia Woolf?* and

the Patterns of History." *ETJ*, 25 (March 1973): 46–52.

The play is an historical allegory on the disappointment and failure of America to maintain a perfect nation.

466. Hopkins, Anthony. "Conventional Albee: *Box* and *Chairman Mao*." *MD*, 16 (Sept. 1973): 141–147.

The box is a recurring image and represents a decaying environment. *Mao's* female characters are typical Albee females, but Chairman Mao is a departure. All of the characters, however represent Albee's conventional comment on the decline of values and morals.

467. Hopper, Stanley Romaine. "How People Live Without Gods: Albee's *Tiny Alice*." *American Poetry Review*, 2 (March-April 1973): 35–38.

Albee has attempted to translate medieval allegorical drama into contemporary terms. Characters and situation contain mystery, morality, and allegorical elements.

468. Jackson, Esther M. "American Theater in the Sixties." *P*, Summer 1973, pp. 236–249.

Albee and playwrights of the 1960s emerge as "the reformers of mankind." *ZS, BS,* and *SB* "are...dramatic representations of interior conflict, studies of those states of anxiety which the romantic philosopher Friedrich Hegel described as 'crises of spirit.' " Albee's language is akin to American drama of the Thirties and Forties.

469. Kingsley, Lawrence. "Reality and Illusion: A Con-

tinuity of a Theme in Albee." *ETJ*, 25 (March 1973): 71–79.

Characters in *ZS, AD, VW, TA,* and *DB* escape into "an Apollonian realm of illusion, from which a Dionysiac annihilation must return them [to reality]."

470. Kolin, Phillip. "A Supplementary Edward Albee Checklist." *S*, 10 (Spring 1973): 28–39.

The bibliography contains 304 primary and secondary sources on Albee up to *AO* (1971) in America and abroad and updates his previous checklist (see no. 330).

471. Lenz, Harold. "At Sixes and Sevens—A Modern Theatrical Structure." *ForumH*, 11 (Summer-Fall 1973 and Winter 1974): 73–79.

The pattern of seven character dramas, as seen in *AO* is a representation of "mankind in seven standard types." *AO* is a morality play on family life.

472. Morsberger, Robert E. "The Movie Game in *Who's Afraid of Virginia Woolf?* and *The Boys in the Band*." *Cos*, 8 (1973): 89–100.

Movie trivia in both plays is used to "show up or put down." In addition, allusions to movies *Beyond the Forest, A Streetcar Named Desire,* and *Bringing Up Baby* and the Walt Disney song "Who's Afraid of the Big Bad Wolf?" are significant to character and thematic analysis.

473. Nilan, Mary M. "Albee's *The Zoo Story:* Alienated Man and the Nature of Love." *MD*, 16 (June 1973): 55–59.

Jerry's failure to find love is rooted in his inability to relate, feel, and give selfless love—a predicament of modern man. Thus, alienation leads to violence as a means of contact.

474. Paolucci, Anne. "Shakespeare and the Genius of the Absurd." *CD*, 7 (Fall 1973): 231–246.

Albee and Shakespeare show "the absurdity of the human condition" through tragic heroic figures, "assertion of human freedom and predestined fate," light and dark imagery, and subtle allegory. *ZS* thru *AO* are cited.

475. Sayre, Nora. "Screen: Albee's *A Delicate Balance*." *NYT*, 11 Dec. 1973, p. 52.

The script and direction are the major faults in this unsuccessful screen adaptation of *DB*.

476. Schneider, Ruth Morris. "The Interpolated Narrative in Modern Drama." Ph.D. dissertation, State University of New York, Albany, 1973. Abstracted in *DA*, 34 (1974): 6605A.

ZS, Hampton's *The Philanthropist*, Pinter's *The Homecoming*, Beckett's *Endgame*, and Ionesco's *The Chairs* use interpolated narrative to shed "thematic light" and "a framework of emotion." Jerry's parable creates tension which offers final enlightenment.

477. Sykes, Carol A. "Albee's Beast Fables: *The Zoo Story* and *A Delicate Balance*." *ETJ*, 25 (Dec. 1973): 448–455.

Jerry's dog story in *ZS* and Tobias' cat story in *DB* are concerned with the inability to communicate. The plays approach the subject differently: "*A Delicate Balance* deals with people's isolation, their resistance to making contact with others, but differs from *Zoo Story* in that it centers on people's pretense that their empty relationships with others are really meaningful." Albee's viewpoint has become more pessimistic for indifference (the dog) lives while truth (the cat) is killed.

478. Taylor, Charlene M. "Coming of Age in New Carthage: Albee's Grown-up Children." *ETJ*, 25 (March 1973): 53–65.

An analysis of imagery and illusion in *VW* "suggests that Albee takes George and Martha through a kind of rite of passage into full adulthood." This "coming of age" theme is exemplified through language that is naturalistic, childish, and heavy in metaphor and allusion.

479. Vos, Nelvin. "The Process of Dying in the Plays of Edward Albee." *ETJ*, 25 (March 1973): 80–85.

The allusions to themes of death and dying in *AO*, *SB*, *EG*, *TA*, *DB*, and *AD* function as a means of communication, self-knowledge, sacrificial love, and indifference.

480. Wallace, Robert S. "*The Zoo Story:* Albee's Attack on Fiction." *MD*, 16 (June 1973): 49–54.

Albee maintains audience objectiveness through "deceptively fictitious" characters and language. Thus, he denies "the use of fiction as a substitute for real experience."

481. White, James E. " 'Santayanian Finesse' in Albee's *Tiny Alice*." *NCL*, 3 (1973): 12–13.

Annotated Bibliography 1968 – 1977 101

> The Lawyer's story of a sonnet he wrote in school is an allusion to Albee's early poem "Nihilist." The passage defines the Lawyer's character and function, methods, and manner.

482. Wilson, Garff B. *Three Hundred Years of American Drama and Theatre,* pp. 486–488. Englewood Cliffs, N.J.: Prentice-Hall, 1973.

> The entry includes a biography and a brief discussion of plays up to *EG* with particular emphasis on *VW* and *TA.*

483. Wilson, Raymond, J. "Transactional Analysis and Literature." Ph.D. dissertation, University of Nebraska, Lincoln, 1973. Abstracted in *DA,* 34 (1974): 7793A.

> Eric Berne's transactional analysis of psychological games is useful for understanding the games in *VW.*

1974

484. Allen, Rex Eugene. "A Production and Production Book of Edward Albee's *A Delicate Balance."* M.A. thesis, Baylor University, 1974.

485. Baker, Burton. "Edward Albee's Nihilistic Plays." Ph.D. dissertation, University of Wisconsin, Madison, 1974. Abstracted in *DA,* 35 (1974): 5387.

> The study examines "themes, characterizations and dramatic forms" of *SB, AD, VW, TA, DB, AO, M,* and *SC* for their affinity with European nihilists, particularly Beckett.

486. Berger, Jere Schindel. "The Rites of Albee." Ph.D. dissertation, Carnegie-Mellon University, 1974.

487. Bierhaus, E.G., Jr. "Strangers in a Room: *A Delicate Balance* Revisited." *MD*, 17 (June 1974): 199–206.

   An analysis of character names and permutations, and the story of Tobias and the cat reveal the universal theme of "dependents seeking 'relief'" from chaos through the denial of order and individuality.

488. Clurman, Harold. *The Divine Pastime: Theatre Essays.* New York: Macmillan, 1974.

   Reprints of reviews of *ZS*, *AD*, and *BS* (1961), *VW* (1962), and *TA* (1965) are located on pp. 107–118. A review of *AO* (1971) is reprinted on pp. 267–272.

489. Finnigan, Jacqueline S. "Protestation Against Progress and Confrontation of Reality: A Study of Dramatic Experimentation in Two Plays by Edward Albee [*ZS* and *TA*]." M.A. thesis, McNeese State College (Louisiana), 1974.

490. Garza, Esmeralda. "A Production and Production Book of Edward Albee's *The Ballad of the Sad Cafe.*" M.F.A. thesis, University of Texas, Austin, 1974.

491. Guernsey, Otis L., ed. *BP of 1973–1974*. New York: Dodd, Mead, 1974.

   Notes and statistics on Albee's plays produced in regional theaters are listed throughout.

492. Lazier, Gil, Douglas Zahn, and Joseph Bellinghiere. "Empirical Analysis of Dramatic Structure." *Speech Monographs,* 41 (Nov. 1974): 381–390.

   A study conducted on a controlled group of students

who saw, read, or read and saw *ZS* revealed "that more exposure to a play produces more agreement upon dramatic structure (as operationalized in this study), and further that this agreement seems to be higher upon reading than upon seeing."

493. McCants, Sarah Maxine. "The Shade and the Mask: Death and Illusion in the Works of Edward Albee." Ph.D. dissertation, University of Southern Mississippi, 1974. Abstracted in *DA*, 35 (1975): 6722A.

    Characters in *ZS*, *SB*, *AD*, *BS*, *VW*, and *TA* "are nonetheless products of a *Weltanschauung* in which dead traditions and static institutions produce alienation and futility." With the exception of *TA*, "the Albeean protagonist seeks to escape his own Death-in-Life situation by destroying those illusions constituent to his spiritual sterility."

494. Moses, Robbie Jeannette Odom. "The Theme of Death in the Plays of Edward Albee." Ph.D. dissertation, University of Houston, 1974. Abstracted in *DA*, 35 (1975): 4443A.

    "This study demonstrates that death permeates his plays, that Albee uses death as both fact and metaphor, and death is the unifying theme in the thirteen plays." *ZS* through *AD* are analyzed.

495. Neblett, Joseph M. "From Stage to Film: A Study of Mike Nichols' *Who's Afraid of Virginia Woolf?*" M.A. thesis, University of Mississippi, 1974.

496. Quinn, James P. "Myth and Romance in Albee's *Who's Afraid of Virginia Woolf?*" *AQ*, 30 (Autumn 1974): 197–204.

Albee parodies conventional romantic myth to attack "all the illusions man has erected to escape the existential burden of his freedom and loneliness...."

497. Smith, Bruce Marc. "Edward Albee's Nuclear Family." M.A. thesis, University of California, Santa Barbara, 1974.

1975

498. Barnes, Clive. "Albee's *Seascape* Is a Major Event." *NYT*, 27 Jan. 1975. Reprinted in *NYTCR*, 1975, p. 368.

The Broadway production is light-hearted with heavy overtones. Albee's compassion gives the play humor and optimism. His first directorial effort is skillful. Cast, costumes, and set are commendable.

499. Beaufort, John. "New Albee Comedy on Broadway." *CSM*, 30 Jan. 1975. Reprinted in *NYTCR*, 1975, p. 371.

SS is "provocative and tantalizing rather than profound...." The first act is boring, the second more enjoyable. Acting, particularly Langella, costuming, and set are good.

500. Bigsby, C.W.E., ed. *Edward Albee: A Collection of Critical Essays*. Englewood Cliffs, N.J.: Prentice-Hall, 1975.

Articles by Gerald Weales (1969, see no. 354), Martin Esslin, Brian Way (1967, see no. 255), Rose Zimbardo (1962), Gilbert Debusscher (1967), Richard Schechner (1963 and 1965), Alan Schneider (1963), Harold Clurman (1966), Diana Trilling (1963), Michael E. Rutenberg (1969, see no. 343), Henry Hewes (1965 and 1971, see no. 396), Philip Roth (1965), Abraham

N. Franzblau (1965), R.S. Stewart (1965), Bigsby (1969, see no. 304), Robert Brustein (1966), and Anne Paolucci (1972, see no. 451) are reprinted. Two new articles by Bigsby are included: *"Box* and *Quotations from Chairman Mao Tse-Tung:* Albee's Diptych," and "To the Brink of the Grave: Edward Albee's *All Over."* Plays treated in the collection are all of Albee's plays up to *AO* with brief mention of *SB, M,* and *EG*. A selected bibliography 1963–1972 and a chronology of important dates 1928–1975 are included.

501. Bogart, Gary. "Elderly Books for Youngerly Readers." *Wilson Library Bulletin*, 50 (Dec. 1975): 315.

    The book reveiw of *SS* finds it Albee's most "lucid" and "optimistic" piece and recommends it for most high school libraries.

502. Brand, Patricia Ann. "Decline and Decay in the Plays of Edward Albee." Ph.D. dissertation, New York University, 1975. Abstract in *DA*, 36 (1975): 3708A.

    ZS, BS, FY, SB, AD, VW, TA, DB, BM, AO, and *SS* are analyzed in light of Oswald Spengler's *The Decline of the West*.

503. Buck, Richard M. *LJ*, 100 (15 June 1975): 1236.

    Albee's *SS* is an "evolutionary parable of the human condition" which is "stretched too thin."

504. Clurman, Harold. "Theatre." *N*, 15 March 1975, p. 314.

    SS is Albee's first "charming" play and denotes a departure from "frustration and venom." The effect of the Broadway production is lessened by the size of the theater. Langella and Anderman are more charming than their human counterparts because of their parts as lizards.

505. Coale, Sam. "The Visions of Edward Albee." *PJ*, 28 Dec. 1975. Reprinted in *NBL,* 95 (Nov.–Dec. 1975): A3.

Albee's language in *AO* and *SS* has become "less flashy . . . Albee may have sacrificed his 'bitchy' vitality in his language but he seems to have discovered a quieter depth, the need to penetrate more ordinary surfaces." *SS* "reveals a newer delightful Albee" optimistic about the future.

506. Coe, Richard M. "Beyond Absurdity: Albee's Awareness of Audience in *Tiny Alice.*" *MD,* 18 (Dec. 1975): 371–383.

Albee has made absurdism "more accessible to general audiences" in *ZS, SB, VW,* and *BM.* Albee's communicative technique, however, is most successful in *TA.*

507. Crosland, Philip F. "*Seascape* Splashes But Hits No High-Water Mark." *Wilmington Evening Journal* (Delaware), 2 Jan. 1975. Reprinted in *NBPA,* 12 (Jan.–Feb. 1975): G14.

The pre-Broadway tryout at Philadelphia's Forrest Theater is a "fascinatingly disappointing" play in which Albee "gives us a lesson in communication and prejudice. . . . Too often, however the talk is surface banter, . . ." Langella's acting, costumes, and setting are particularly effective.

508. Eichelbaum, Stanley. "An Incendiary *Alice* Returns."

SFE, 6 Oct. 1975. Reprinted in *NBPA*, 68 (Sept.–Oct.): D7.

William Ball's production at the ACT was "deplored" by Albee. Ball's editing of the third act, however, was necessary. The cast is not as polished as ACT's previous revivals, but direction is constant and settings and lighting are good.

509. Gill, Brendan. "The Theatre." *NY*, 3 Feb. 1975, pp. 75–76.

"Of all Mr. Albee's plays *Seascape* is the most exquisitely written." Kerr, Langella and Anderman give notable performances, Tilton's scenery is "utterly convincing," and the costumes are "ingenious."

510. Gottfried, Martin. "Theater." *NYP*, 22 Jan. 1975. Reprinted in *NYTCR*, 1975, p. 369.

SS is lifeless and void of humanity. The dialogue is stilted and does not allow the actors to relate to each other nor to the audience.

511. Guernsey, Otis L., ed. *BP of 1974–1975*. New York: Dodd, Mead, 1975.

Albee is mentioned throughout with production notes and statistics of his plays produced in regional theater, a synopsis of *SS*, A Best Play selection (pp. 213–227), and awards won for the year.

512. Hewes, Henry. "Theater." *SR*, 8 March 1975, p. 40.

In *SS*, "Albee seems to be suggesting that the real solution is for our civilization to recognize its failures and somehow to feed our experiences into the evolution of a new and bettter species." His "exquisite concern for the careful use of language" compensates for the "lack of dramatic urgency" in the first act. The ending is optimistic and augurs the retirement years as a time of teaching future generations. The casting of Kerr and Nelson is questionable, but Langella is exceptional. Acting, sets, and costumes maintain the absurd and fantastic atmosphere.

513. Higgins, John. "Edward Albee's Lesson from the Lizards." *LT,* 30 Jan. 1975, p. 8.

"*Seascape* finds Albee in a cool and crisp, humane mood." The play "is about not closing down when you are getting on." Plaudits go to the cast, particularly Langella.

514. Hill, Linda M. "Language as Aggression: Studies in Postwar Drama." Ph.D. dissertation, Yale, 1975. Abstracted in *DA,* 35 (1975): 4524A. Published in Bonn, Ger.: Bouvier Verlag Herbert Grundmann, 1976.

AD is one of the absurdist plays which "associate cruelty and treachery through language with a national, cultural, or class tradition."

515. Hughes, Catherine. "Albee's *Seascape*" *AM,* 22 Feb. 1975, pp. 136–137. Reprinted in *PP,* May 1975, pp. 34–35.

The play lacks life and is artificial in comparison to *VW* and *ZS.* Albee's direction "makes its failure even more regrettable."

516. Hull, Elizabeth Anne. "A Transactional Analysis of the Plays of Edward Albee." Ph.D. dissertation, Loyola University (Chicago), 1975. Abstracted in *DA*, 36 (1975): 313A.

Transactional analysis is employed to explore psychological realism in *ZS, BS, SB, AD, VW, SC, M, DB, ED, BM,* and *AO.*

517. "In *Seascape* Albee Is in Trim Again." *Philadelphia Inquirer*, 5 Jan. 1975. Reprinted in *NBPA*, 13 (Jan.–Feb. 1975): A5.

"The dialogue is spare and engaging, the play gains impetus and clout" in the pre-Broadway tryout of *SS* at the Forrest Theater in Philadelphia. Some ideas, however, need further development.

518. Johnson, Malcolm L. "Albee's Difficult *All Over.*" *HC*, 9 Nov. 1975. Reprinted in *NBPA*, 84 (Nov.–Dec. 1975): C7–8.
"*All Over* is a flawed and difficult work and the Hartford Stage Company production has neither improved on it, nor made it easier." The Mistress is the only full-developed character. The play's themes are not illuminated and the wordplay does not enhance characterization. The company has lost the force and satire of the piece.

519. Kalem, T.E. "The Theater." *T*, 10 Feb. 1975. Reprinted in *NYTCR*, 1975, p. 372.

SS "is bland and innocuous" like all of Albee's works since *VW*. The Broadway cast, however, is good.

520. Kauffman, Stanley. "On Theater." *NewR*, 22 Feb. 1975, p. 22.

   SS is banal because the idea of middle-age self-evaluation is never developed fully and the play offers no statement. Albee should consider switching professions, possibly to criticism. As a director of the Broadway production, he achieves "very mixed results." Acting and costumes are commendable.

521. Kissel, Howard, "Seascape." *WWD*, 27 Jan. 1975. Reprinted in *NYTCR*, 1975, p. 370.

   SS is similar to *VW* in that an older couple instructs a younger couple by means of an outburst and violence. *SS*, however, is less significant. The dialogue is more amusing than pretentious. The onstage fantasy, though never fully developed, is the most refreshing feature. Overall, the absurdist technique of "indefiniteness" hampers the script.

522. Kroll, Jack. "Theater." *NW*, 10 Feb. 1975, p. 75. Reprinted in *NYTCR*, 1975, pp. 372–373.

   Albee envisions a decaying civilization whose only hope is to be re-populated with sea creatures. Pretentious language has become Albee's downfall over the years.

523. Loeffler, Donald L. *An Analysis of the Treatment of the Homosexual Character in Dramas Produced in the New York Theatre from 1950 to 1968*. New York: Arno Press, 1975.

   Homosexual implications in *AD*, *SC*, *M*, *TA*, and *ZS* are briefly discussed throughout.

524. Loynd, Ray. "Albee's View from the Sea." *Herald Examiner* (Los Angeles), 4 April 1975. Reprinted in *NBPA*, 28 (March–April 1975): E1.

   SS should not be "over intellectualized" or "analyzed" too deeply. Nelson's performance overshadows Kerr's in the Los Angeles production. Langella gives "a knockout performance" and Anderman, set, lighting, and costumes are commendable.

525. Miller, Joanne. " 'Once you stop trying to figure it out. . . .' " *SFE*, 19 Sept. 1975. Reprinted in *NBPA*, 68 (Sept.–Oct. 1975): D6.

   William Ball, general director of ACT in San Francisco, comments on his revival of *TA*. Willis and Cortland who will play Miss Alice and Julian, respectively, discuss abstraction and their roles in the play.

526. Moses, Robbie. "Edward Albee: A Voice in the Wasteland." *ForumH*, 12 (Winter 1975): 35–40.

   Albee's plays are preoccupied with death, particularly with those people "who *are* dead to life." Albee's "adaptation of the Christian equation of love and death" gives his plays religious overtones. "Death, for Albee is a metaphor for affirming life lived honestly, courageously, and abundantly within the human condition encompassing the temporal and the eternal, the sacred and the profane."

527. Probst, Leonard. *"Seascape."* NBC, 27 Jan. 1975. Reprinted in *NYTCR*, 1975, p. 373.

   The Broadway production is "pretentious." The set and dialogue recall Beckett. "It is a stylized, well-acted, well-staged zero."

528. Sanders, Kevin. "*Seascape.*" *WABC-TV* 7, 26 Jan. 1975. Reprinted in *NYTCR*, 1975, p. 373.

> The Broadway production is enigmatic but not profound. The dialogue is trivial and the situation contrived.

529. Sapoznik, Ran. "The One-Act Plays of Thornton Wilder, William Saroyan and Edward Albee." Ph.D. dissertation, University of Kansas, 1975. Abstracted in *DA*, 37 (1976): 700A.

> The purpose of the study is "to initiate inquiry into the dramatic and theatrical means used by playwrights since the 1920s to express their themes within the form of a one-act play."

530. Stavrou, C.N. "Albee in Wonderland." *Southwest Review*, 60 (Winter 1975): 46–61.

> Albee's condemns man's illusions, technocracy, and conformity and questions familial ties in *ZS*, *BS*, *SB*, *AD*, *TA*, *VW*, and *BM*. He is a social critic warning man to "dive in or courageously build anew on the precipice's edge."

531. Simon, John. "Evolution Made Queasy." *NYM*, 10 Feb. 1975, p. 55.

> The Broadway production of *SS* is a "simple-minded allegory" replete with "doughy verbiage, feebly quivering inaction, and grandly gesticulating pretentiousness."

532. Smith, Rebecca Louise. "Dissonance as Method in the Plays of Edward Albee." Ph.D. dissertation, University of Alberta (Canada), 1975.

533. Taylor, Robert. "Albee's *Tiny Alice* by ACT: Overwritten, Underwrought." *OT*, 7 Oct. 1975. Reprinted in *NBPA*, 68 (Sept–Oct. 1975): D8.

Albee's complaints on the show will make it successful. Ball's direction gives "dramatic life to this overwritten, ultimately disappointing work. . . ." Ball's third revival of the play is "not so dynamic" because of cast and "underwrought" direction.

534. "Upbeat Albee—His Best in Years." *SFE*, 2 March 1975. Reprinted in *NBPA*, 28 (March–April): E2.

"The play [*SS*] is witty, stimulating, deceptively simple allegory that examines the merits of evolution, or change, in a world bogged down by bias and inertia." The opening scene is slow, but the second act is "a delightful comedy of manners." Langella is outstanding and costumes and set are commendable.

535. Watt, Douglas. "*Seascape:* The Lizard Has the Lines." *NYDN*, 27 Jan. 1975. Reprinted in *NYTCR*, 1975, p. 369.

The play is "more literary than dramatic . . . a staged short story." The allegory is suggestive of Beckett. Langella is the Broadway production's highlight.

536. Wilson, Edwin. "Disturbing Creatures of the Deep." *WSJ*, 28 Jan. 1975. Reprinted in *NYTCR*, 1975, p. 370.

The introduction of the lizards into the first act would have eased the tediousness. Albee raises many questions about evolution that are never answered.

1976

537. Barnes, Clive. "Stage: *Virginia Woolf*." *NYT*, 2 April 1976. Reprinted in *NYTCR*, 1976, p. 310.

Albee's direction of the Broadway revival emphasizes the humor and heterosexuality and increases the pace. Thus, the play emerges less mysterious and symbolic.

538. Beaufort, John. "*Who's Afraid of Virginia Woolf?* Is Potent Revival." *CSM*, 9 April 1976. Reprinted in *NYTCR*, 1976, p. 313.

The Broadway production is a comedy with hints of allegory concerning our society. The performances are good.

539. Brody, Benjamin. "Psychology and the Arts." *Psychology Today*, Oct. 1976, p. 26.

VW "is a classic exposition of trends of the American national character." The Broadway revival "is constructed expertly, performed by superb actors, and mounted in a definitive production directed by the author himself." The homosexual family structure within the play "pushes his [Albee's] vision of sterility to its biological and symbolic ultimate."

540. Fodor, Jean Roberta. "The Importance of the Female in the Plays of Samuel Beckett, Harold Pinter, and Edward Albee." Ph.D. dissertation, University of Washington, 1976. Abstracted in *DA*, 37 (1977): 1378A.

Albee's women—Grandma in *AD*, Martha in *VW*, Agnes in *DB*, and The Wife in *AO*—like Pinter's women, are less pessimistic than Beckett's females. Albee and Pinter's characters make an effort to transcend modern chaos.

541. Gabbard, Lucinda P. "At the Zoo: From O'Neill to Albee." *MD*, 19 (Dec. 1976): 365–374.

ZS and *The Hairy Ape* are compared and contrasted.

542. Gale, William. "*Virginia Woolf* Still Has Same Bite." *PJ*, 10 Feb. 1976. Reprinted in *NBPA*, 29 (March–April 1976): F10.

    "The revival of *Virginia Woolf* at the Colonial in Boston is an excellent production, beautifully timed, well-acted, and closely balanced with the humor and horror of this landmark play intact." Ben Gazzara is particularly good.

543. Getlein, Frank. "PBS' *All Over* Has Everything But a Play." *Washington Star* (D.C.), 28 April 1976. Reprinted in *NBFTV*, 31 (May–June 1976): A5–6.

    The Theater in America production features "excellent" acting, directing, and setting. The script, however, has no "dramatic conflict" and "nothing is sustained. . . . All this inaction is made worse by verse."

544. Gill, Brendan. "The Theatre." *NY*, 12 April 1976, p. 101.

    The Broadway production of *VW* is an "admirable revival." Dewhurst and Gazzara "rise to stunning effect" but Kelton and Anderman are disappointing. Albee's direction is questionable in the handling of liquor and the slow, unrealistic pace of the ending.

545. Gottfried, Martin. "*Woolf* Returns with Same Bite." *NYP*, 2 April 1976. Reprinted in *NYTCR*, 1976, p. 311.

    VW is a classic because its theatrical power hasn't diminished over the years. The play, however, leaves many questions unanswered. The Broadway revival is well acted and directed.

546. Guernsey, Otis L., ed. *BP of 1975–1976*. New York: Dodd, Mead, 1976.

Notes on the revivals of *AO* at the Hartford Stage Company and *VW* on Broadway are featured on pp. 58 and 346, respectively. Regional theater productions of Albee plays are also noted.

547. Hempel, Peter, "From 'Survival Kit' to *Seascape:* Edward Albee's Evolutionary Drama." Ph.D. dissertation, University of Texas, Austin, 1976. Abstracted in *DA*, 36 (1976): 6683.

Albee's moral vision contends that in political terms man can free himself from the daily routine and in evolutionary terms, man can overcome physical evolution "through the medium of culture and the development of civilization." Albee's plays through *SS* are discussed.

548. Hughes, Catherine. "Edward Albee," pp. 52–63. In *American Playwrights—1945–1975*. Bath, Eng.: Pitman, 1976.

Criticism of *ZS, AD, TA, DB, SS,* and *AO* previously published in *AM* and *PP* is reprinted. Overall, Albee's style has been disappointing since *VW* and *ZS*.

549. ———. "Truth, Illusion and *Virginia Woolf*." *AM*, 24 April 1976, pp. 362–363.

The Broadway revival reinforces *VW* as Albee's best play and "almost unquestionably the major theatrical experience provided by an American writer of Albee's generation."

550. Irwin, Robert. "The 'Teaching Emotion' in the Ending of *The Zoo Story*." *NCL*, 6 (1976): 6–8.

Jerry combines kindness and cruelty with the dog and Peter "to achieve the contact he needs" at least once before he dies and "to produce the 'teaching emotion.'"

551. Kalem, T.E. "The Theater." *T*, 12 April 1976, pp. 82–83. Reprinted in *NYTCR*, 1976, p. 313.

    The Broadway revival of *VW* is humorous and triumphant, and the actors are good.

552. Kissel, Howard. *"Who's Afraid of Virginia Woolf?" WWD*, 2 April 1976. Reprinted in *NYTCR*, 1976, p. 312.

    Familiarity with the play now makes the Broadway revival more enjoyable. The play "has the air of a classical comedy."

553. Kroll, Jack. "Theater." *NW*, 12 April 1976, p. 109. Reprinted in *NYTCR*, 1976, p. 312.

    The Broadway production of *VW* is a "superb revival," and the work remains the author's best to date. The production is staged more like "social comedy" than the original. The imaginary child "seems less bizarre and problematic." The acting is excellent.

554. La Belle, Jenijoy. "Albee's *Who's Afraid of Virginia Woolf?*" *Ex*, 35 (Fall 1976): 8–9.

    George and Martha are akin to the title couple in Virginia Woolf's short story "Lappin and Lapinova." Ernest and George "kill" the fictional rabbit and child, respectively, upon which their childless marriages are based. Rosalind and Martha fear facing life without illusions.

555. Moses, Robbie Odom. "Death as a Mirror of Life: Edward Albee's *All Over.*" *MD*, 19 (March 1976): 67–77.

The death of the man brings to the surface social issues concerning death and dying. Also, "death is a mirror reflecting family ties built upon rancor, resentment, and rivalry."

556. Mullin, Donald. "The 'Decline of the West' as Reflected in Three Modern Plays." *ETJ*, 28 (Oct. 1976): 363–365.

"The lesson they [the characters in *BM*] all finally understand is the same put forward in *The Dog Beneath the Skin* and *Romulus the Great:* Middle-class institutions and life habits are meaningless, self-centered, frequently cruel, and all to no apparent purpose." Albee sees change as "an almost assured promise of a renewed series of mistakes in essentially the same old format."

557. O'Connor, John. "TV: A Superb Production of Albee's *All Over.*" *NYT*, 28 April 1976, p. 83.

Aired 28 April 1976 as a part of the Theater in America series, the play is "not precise but self-conscious." The production is "performed to perfection," however.

558. Sanders Kevin. *"Who's Afraid of Virginia Woolf?"* WABC-TV 7, 1 April 1976. Reprinted in *NYTCR*, 1976, p. 314.

The play is Albee's best and the Broadway revival is good. The script, however, remains "heavily melodramatic" despite good performances.

559. Shorey, Kenneth Paul. "Albee Work Memorable, Acting Superb, Precise." *Birmingham News,* 27 Jan. 1976. Reprinted in *NBFTV,* 4 (Jan.–Feb. 1976): D9.

   The review of the film *DB* states "the craftmanship of Albee's play is something quite rare in modern American letters. . . . It's a hybrid production . . . that inevitably suffers, to some degree, by the placement of a camera lens between performers and audience."

560. Shorter, Eric. "Plays in Performance: Regions." *QTR,* Winter 1976, p. 56.

   The Garden Centre, Brighton revival of *AO* is "elegantly boring but well-acted."

561. Watt, Douglas. "Long Night's Journey into Day." *NYDN,* 2 April 1976. Reprinted in *NYTCR,* 1976, p. 310.

   The Broadway production of *VW* is a "superb revival" whose "shock value" has not diminished. The play remains a masterpiece of American theater.

562. Watts, Richard. "*Virginia Wolff* [sic] a Tribute to Albee." *NYP,* 12 April 1976. Reprinted in *NBPA,* 29 (March–April 1976): F11.

   The Broadway revival is "more brilliant than ever. . . . The cast is superior to their predecessors," particularly Ben Gazzara. Though *SS* is Albee's best play, *VW* "is surely his most powerful and steadily fascinating one."

563. Wilson, Edwin. "Sound and Fury in a Living Room," *WSJ,* 7 April 1976. Reprinted in *NYTCR,* 1976, p. 312.

Theatrically, the acting, dialogue, and direction of the Broadway revival of *VW* is entertaining. The themes of the decline of Western civilization, role-playing, and the shattering of illusions, however, are never fully developed and do not relate to each other.

564. Wurster, G.S. "Albee's Festival Chant: *Who's Afraid of Virginia Woolf?*" *Michigan Academician*, 9 (Summer 1976): 61–67.

VW "can be best understood as a theme of sterility played against a countertheme of archetypical fertility rituals with a statement about truth and illusion which is developed by association rather than logical progress." Albee suggests than man creates myths and ritual to create order. The play incorporates rituals and myths from the May Day festivals, *Walpurgisnacht*, Saturn and Dionysus, Christian burial rites, and fertility and sacrificial rites.

1977

565. Barnes, Clive. "Stage: Double Bill by Albee." *NYT*, 4 Feb. 1977, sec. 3, p. 3.

Albee's *CW* and *L* at the Hartford Stage Company have difficulty communicating their message. The plays maintain interest, and Albee's interest in the mechanics of theater is evident.

566. Bennett, Robert. "Tragic Vision in *The Zoo Story*." *MD*, 20 (March 1977): 55–66.

Jerry is a tragic hero and a philosopher who questions "whether spiritual love is a genuine human faculty or an illusion." Like a tragic hero, he searches for "his personal dignity." His "tragic awakening" through

Peter is "an honest attempt to resolve the basic tensions within himself, and by extension within man."

567. *Choice: Books for College Libraries,* 14 (Sept. 1977): 853.

The themes of "love and communication" are placed in Albee's familiar Pinteresque style. "Both [*CW* and *L*] are strong fare, with the usual Albee predilections in play, and both are well worth attending to."

568. Esslin, Martin. *"Counting the Ways." PP,* Feb. 1977, p. 33.

CW at the National Theatre, London should be played in a smaller theater and with *L*. *CW* is "a very brilliant piece of miniature painting" in which traditional themes of love and marriage "are tackled in novel and original ways, in a splendid, if somewhat mannerist style." Reid and Gough are "first rate."

569. Guernsey, Otis L., ed. *BP of 1976–1977.* New York: Dodd, Mead, 1977.

Notes on the American premiere of *CW* and *L* at the Hartford Stage Company (p. 64) and other Albee productions at regional theaters are featured throughout.

570. Johnson, Malcolm L. "Albee Mixes Humor, Pain." *HC,* 3 Feb. 1977. Reprinted in *NBPA,* 11 (Jan.–Feb. 1977): B12.

"Each of the plays [*CW* and *L*] has its own strength, though neither seems likely to be ranked among Albee's major works. But the playwright has directed them with cogency and skill and his cast of three . . .

give precise, persuasive performances," particularly Anderman. Costumes, lighting, and setting "help to endow these plays with resonance and reality."

571. Johnson, Malcolm L. "Albee Directs Albee." *HC*, 6 Feb. 1977. Reprinted in *NBPA*, 11 (Jan.–Feb. 1977): B11.

Albee is "a lucid and deliberate director." *CW* and *L* "are concerned with individual isolation, and the impermanence of love, perhaps even the possibility of it." Death also permeates both plays. The actors, costumes, settings, and lighting are commendable.

572. *Kirkus Reviews*, 45 (1 April 1977): 410.

A review of the book finds *CW*'s "glacial He-and-She" akin to Albee's other married couples. Their marital bouts are "meticulously programmed for performance—with detailed, eloquent, parenthetical directions that attest to the canniness of the Albee ear." *L* is less interesting and recalls "Albee-the-obscurantist."

573. Kroll, Jack. "Theater." *NW*, 14 Feb. 1977, p. 69.

Albee's "mulling over other artists and thinkers" is "a lethal substitute for experience." His limitation of Auden in *CW* is full of "gimpy aphorisms" and an unsuccessful attempt "to express agonies and ironies of our disaffected spirits...." *L* "is maddeningly uselessly obscure and evasive." Albee's "gift" lies not in language but in "capturing the cries, whispers, and snarls of wounded human animals."

574. Mah, Kai-Ho-. "Albee's *Who's Afraid of Virginia Woolf?*" *Ex*, 35 (Summer 1977): 10–11.

George's phrase "ice for the lamps of China, Manchuria thrown in" refers to oriental lamps that revolve and give the illusion of running horses. This "circle-cyclic motif runs throughout the play certainly in the characters' lives," their drinking habits, and their childish songs.

575. Page, Michael. *LJ*, 102 (15 May 1977): 1204.

The book review finds *CW* "precisely formal and delightfully human." *L*, however, is a continuance of Albee's preoccupation with language and would seem dull for the stage.

576. Rogoff, Gordon. "Theater." *SR*, 2 April 1977, pp. 36–37.

CW and *L* at the Hartford Stage Company "under the author's flaccid direction, are about people without names, hiding behind a language without passion. . . . Neither play makes much of plot or character." Influences of Pinter, Brecht, and Pirandello are apparent. Language is both plays' chief fault, though "Albee has released some tenderness between He and She that I don't recall in his other plays."

577. Watt, Douglas. "A Long Night of Albee." *NYDN*, 5 Feb. 1977. Reprinted in *NBPA*, 11 (Jan.–Feb. 1977): B10.

The Hartford Stage Company productions of *CW* and *L* "revealed themselves as near-lifeless disappointments . . . form seems more and more to dominate content so that love and its infinite variations, one of the playwright's major concerns, are here imprisoned in a kind of cloudy aspic, increasingly dense as the evening which he himself has staged, wears on."

CW has "a certain cuteness, even silliness" and "a morbid air." *L* is "an increasingly tedious and obscure songfest."

No Date

578. Gilmore, S. "Modern American Drama with Special Reference to the Works of Edward Albee." M. Litt., Glasgow (Eng.), n.d.

579. Willis, Mrs. N.J. "The Treatment of the Family in the Plays of Eugene O'Neill, Tennessee Williams and Edward Albee." Ph.D., London, R.H.C., n.d.

Library Resources
Consulted

Library Resources Consulted

BIBLIOGRAPHIES OF BIBLIOGRAPHIES

General

Altick, Richard Daniel, and Andrew H. Wright. *Selective Bibliography for the Study of English and American Literature.* 5th ed. New York: Macmillan, 1975.
Bibliographic Index: A Cumulative Bibliography of Bibliographies [1937—] New York: H.W. Wilson, 1938—.
Besterman, Theodore. *Literature, English and American: A Bibliography of Bibliographies.* Totowa, N.J.: Rowman and Littlefield, 1971.
———. *A World Bibliography of Bibliographies and of Bibliographical Catalogues, Calendars, Abstracts, Digests, Indexes, and the Like.* 4th ed., rev. and enl. 5 vols. Lausanne: Societas Bibliographica, 1965–1966.
Brockett, Oscar G., Samuel L. Becker, and Donald C. Bryant. *A Bibliographical Guide to Research in Speech and Dramatic Art.* Chicago: Scott, 1963.

British

The British National Bibliography [1950—]. London: The Council of the British National Bibliography, Ltd. 1951—.

BOOK LISTS AND RECORDS OF PUBLICATION

Books in Print. New York: R.R. Bowker, 1948–.
British Books in Print. London: Whittaker, 1874—.
Cumulative Book Index [1898]. New York: H.W. Wilson, 1900—.
The National Union Catalog: A Cumulative Author List. Washington: Library of Congress, 1956—.

NEWSPAPERS, MAGAZINES, AND MISCELLANEOUS INDEXES

Newspaper Directories

Newsbank Review of the Arts: Film and Television. Greenwich, Conn.: Newsbank, Inc., 1975—.
Newsbank Review of the Arts: Literature. Greenwich, Conn.: Newsbank, Inc., 1975—
Newsbank Review of the Arts: Performing Arts. Greenwich, Conn.: Newsbank, Inc., 1975—.
The New York Times Directory of the Theater. New York: New York Times Book Co. and Arno Press, 1973.
The New York Times Index. New York: New York Times Company, 1913—.
The New York Times Theater Reviews [1920]. New York: The New York Times Book Co. and Arno Press, 1971—.
Times Index [1906—.]. Reading. Eng.: Newspaper Archives Developments, Ltd., 1907—.

Periodicals

American Humanities Index [1975—]. Troy, N.Y.: Whitston, 1976—.

"Articles in American Studies [1954—]." *American Quarterly,* 7 (1955).
"Articles on American Literature Appearing in Current Periodicals." *American Literature: A Journal of Literary History, Criticism, and Bibliography.* Durham, N.C.: Duke University Press, 1929—.
Book Review Digest. New York: H.W. Wilson, 1905—.
Book Review Index. Detroit: Gale Research, 1965—.
British Humanities Index (formerly *Subject Index to Periodicals*) [1915—]. London: The Library Assoc., 1919—.
Canadian Periodical Index [1948—]. Ottawa: National Library of Canada, 1950—.
The Catholic Periodical and Literature Index [1930—]. New York Catholic Library Assoc., 1939—.
Current Book Review Citations [1976—]. New York: H.W. Wilson, 1977—.
The Education Index [1929—]. New York: H.W. Wilson, 1932—.
Humanities Index (formerly *The Internaitonal Index* and *Social Sciences and Humanities Index*) [1907—]. New York: H.W. Wilson, 1916—.
Index to Book Reviews in the Humanities. Detroit: Phillip Thompson, 1960—.
Index to Commonwealth Little Magazines [1964]. New York: Johnson Reprint Corp., 1966—.
Index to Little Magazines [1948—]. Denver: Alan Swallow, 1949—.
The International Guide to Literary and Art Periodicals [1960—]. London: Villiers Publications, 1961–1962(?).
Leary, Lewis, comp. *Articles on American Literature 1950–1967.* Durham, N.C.: Duke University Press, 1970.
National Library Service Cumulative Book Review Index 1905–1974. Princeton, N.J.: National Library Service Co., 1975.
Popular Periodical Index [1973—]. Camden, N.J.: Popular Periodical Index, 1974—.
Reader's Guide to Periodical Literature [1900—]. New York: H.W. Wilson, 1901—.

Sader, Marion, ed. *Comprehensive Index to English-Language Little Magazines 1890–1970*, Series One. 8 vols. Millwood, N.Y.: Kraus-Thomson, 1976.

Miscellaneous

Facts on File Yearbook [1941—]. New York: H.W. Wilson, 1942—.

Vertical File Index. New York: H.W. Wilson, 1932—.

DISSERTATIONS, THESES, AND RESEARCH IN PROGRESS

American, General

American Doctoral Dissertations (formerly *Index to American Doctoral Dissertations*), 1955—. Ann Arbor: University Microfilms, 1957—.

Dissertation Abstracts International (formerly *Dissertation Abstracts*) Ann Arbor: University Microfilms, 1938—.

Masters Abstracts. Ann Arbor: University Microfilms, 1962—.

Master's Theses in Education [1951—]. Cedar Falls: Research Publications, 1953—.

Woodress, James. *Dissertations in American Literature, 1891–1966.* Durham, N.C.: Duke University Press, 1968.

American, Speech and Dramatic Art

"Abstracts of Theses in the Field of Speech and Drama." *Speech Monographs,* 13 (1946–1969).

"Doctoral Dissertations in Speech: Work in Progress [1951—]." *Speech Monographs*, 18 (1951—).

Bibliographic Annual in Speech Communication [1969—]. New York: Speech Communication Assoc., 1970—.

"Doctoral Projects in Progress in Theater Arts [1948—]." *Educational Theater Journal*, 1 (1949—).

Knower, Franklin H. "Graduate Theses—An Index of Graduate Work in Speech," *Speech Monographs*, 2 (1935–1969).

———. "Graduate Theses—An Index of Graduate Work in Theatre [1949—]." *Educational Theater Journal*, 3 (1951—).

Litto, Frederic M. *American Dissertations on the Drama and Theatre.* Kent, Ohio: Kent State University Press, 1969.

Foreign

Index to Theses Accepted for Higher Degrees in the Universities of Great Britain and Ireland. London: Aslib, 1953—.

McNamee, Laurence F., ed. *Dissertations in English and American Literature: Theses Accepted by American, British, and German Unversities, 1865–1964.* New York: R.R. Bowker, 1968. Supplement One, 1964–68. New York: R.R. Bowker, 1969. Supplement Two, 1969—73. New York: R.R. Bowker, 1974.

MANUSCRIPTS AND SPECIAL COLLECTIONS IN THE U.S.

The National Union Catalog of Manuscript Collections [1959—]. Washington, D.C.: Library of Congress, 1962—.

Quarterly Journal of Current Acquisitions. Washington, D.C.: Library of Congress, 1943—.

Robbins, Albert, ed. *American Literary Manuscripts: A Checklist of Holdings in Academic, Historical and Public Libraries in the*

United States. 2d ed. Athens: University of Georgia Press, 1977.

Young, William C. *American Theatrical Arts: A Guide to Manuscripts and Special Collections in the United States and Canada.* Chicago: American Library Assoc., 1971.

BIOGRAPHY

Biography Index [1946—]. New York: H.W. Wilson, 1947—.

Biography News. Detroit: Gale Research, 1974–1976.

Chicorel, Marietta, ed. *Chicorel Index to Biographies.* New York: Chircorel Library Publishing Corp., 1974.

Current Biography Yearbook. New York: H.W. Wilson, 1940—.

Havlice, Patricia Pate. *Index to Literary Biography.* 2 vols. Metuchen, N.J.: Scarecrow Press, 1975.

LaBeau, Dennis, and Gary C. Tarbert. *Biographical Dictionaries Master Index 1975–76.* Detroit: Gale Research, 1975.

The New York Times Biographical Service (formerly *The New York Times Biographical Edition*). New York: New York Times, Co., 1970—.

Nicholson, Margaret E. *People in Books.* New York: H.W. Wilson, 1969. *Supplement One.* New York: H.W. Wilson, 1977.

PLAYS IN COLLECTIONS AND PERIODICALS

Chicorel, Marietta, ed. *Chicorel Theater Index to Plays in Anthologies. Periodicals, Discs, and Tapes.* 2 vols. New York: Chicorel Library Publishing Corp., 1970–1971.

———. *Chicorel Theater Index to Plays in Collections, Anthologies, Periodicals, and Discs, in England.* New York: Chicorel Library Publishing Corp., 1972.

———. *Chicorel Theater Index to Plays in Periodicals.* New York: Chicorel Library Publishing Corp., 1973.

Connor, John M., and Billie M. Connor. *Ottemiller's Index to Plays in Collections, and Author and Title Index to Plays Appearing in Collections Published Between 1900 and 1975.* 6th ed., rev. and enl. Metuchen, N.J.: Scarecrow Press, 1976.

Fidell, Estelle., ed. *Play Index.* 4 vols. New York: H.W. Wilson, 1973.

Guernsey, Otis L. *Directory of the American Theater 1874–1971.* New York: Dodd, Mead, 1971.

Logasa, Hannah. *An Index to One-Act Plays for Stage, Radio, and Television,* Fifth Supplement, 1956–1964. Boston: F.W. Faxon, 1966.

Salem, James, ed. *Drury's Guide to Best Plays.* 2d ed. Metuchen, N.J.: Scarecow Press, 1969.

Samples, Gordon. *The Drama Scholar's Index to Plays and Filmscripts: A Guide to Plays and Filmscripts in Selected Anthologies, Series, and Periodicals.* Metuchen, N.J.: Scarecrow Press, 1974.

LITERATURE

General

Abstracts of English Studies. Boulder, Col.: National Council of Teachers of English, 1958—.

Annual Bibliography of English Language and Literature [1920—]. Cambridge, Eng.: Bowes and Bowes, 1921—.

Canadian Essay and Literature Index [1973—]. Toronto: University of Toronto Press, 1975—.

"Current Bibliography [of Twentieth-Century Literature, 1954—]." *Twentieth Century Literature: A Scholarly and Critical Journal,* (1955—).

MLA Abstracts of Articles in Scholarly Journals. New York: New York University Press, 1971—.

MLA International Bibliography of Books and Articles on the Modern Languages and Literatures. New York: New York University Press, 1922—.

Pownall, David E. *Articles on Twentieth Century Literature: An Annotated Bibliography, 1954–1970.* 7 vols. New York: Kraus-Thomson, 1973.

Yearbook of Comparative and General Literature. Bloomington: Indiana University Press, 1952—.

The Year's Work in English Studies [1919—]. London: Oxford University Press, 1921—.

The Year's Work in Modern Language Studies [1929—]. Cambridge, Eng.: The University Press, 1931—.

American

American Literary Scholarship [1963—]. Durham, N.C.: Duke University Press, 1965—.

American Literature Abstracts. Stockton, Calif.: American Literature Abstracts, 1967—.

Blanck, Jacob, comp. *Bibliography of American Literature.* New Haven: Yale University Press, 1955—.

Essay and General Literature Index [1900—]. New York: H.W. Wilson, 1934—.

DRAMA

General

Adelman, Irving, and Rita Dworkin, comps. *Modern Drama: A Checklist of Critical Literature on 20th-Century Plays.* Metuchen, N.J.: Scarecrow Press, 1967.

Chicorel, Marietta, ed. *Chicorel Bibliography to the Performing Arts.* New York: Chicorel Library Publishing Corp., 1972.

Revue d'Histoire du Théâtre. Paris: Brient, 1948—.

Young, William C. "Scholarly Works in Progress." *Educational Theatre Journal,* 26 (1974—).

American

"A Bibliography of Speech and Theatre in the South for the Year [1954—]." *Southern Speech Journal,* 20 (1955—). Later A Bibliography of Speech and Theater and Mass Communication in the South for the Year.

Breed, Paul F., and Florence M. Sniderman, eds. *Dramatic Criticism Index.* Detroit: Gale Research, 1972.

Coleman, Arthur, and Gary R. Tyler. *Drama Criticism.* 2 vols. Denver: A. Swallow, 1966–1971.

Eddelman, Floyd Eugene, comp. *American Drama Criticism Supplement II.* Hamden, Conn.: Shoe String Press, 1976.

Long Eugene H. *American Drama from Its Beginnings to the Present.* New York: Appleton, 1970.

Palmer, Helen H., and Jane Anne Dyson, comps. *American Drama Criticism.* Hamden, Conn.: Shoe String Press,

1967. *Supplement I.* Hamden, Conn.: Shoe String Press, 1970.

Salem, James M. *A Guide to Critical Reviews, Part I: American Drama. 1909–1969.* 2d ed. Metuchen, N. J.; Scarecrow Press, 1973.

APPENDICES

Appendix A

CONTRIBUTING AUTHORS INDEX

Adler, Thomas P. - 457
Agnihotri, S.M. - 435
Allen, Rex E. - 484
Amacher, Richard E. - 458
Anzalone, Frank M. - 220
Argenio, Joseph - 436

Bachman, Charles R. - 437
Baker, Burton - 485
Ballew, Leighton M. - 160, 169, 183
Bannon, Barbara A. - 256, 302
Barnes, Clive - 257, 258, 302, 379, 498, 537, 565
Beaufort, John - 499, 538
Bellinghiere, Joseph - 492
Bennett, Robert - 566
Berger, Jere S. - 486
Bierhaus, E.G. - 487
Bigsby, C.W.E. - 235, 259, 304, 500
Blades, Larry - 381
Borart, Gary - 501
Boros, Donald - 236
Bosworth, Patricia - 127
Bourdonnay, Katherine - 260
Brand, Patricia A. - 502
Bristow, Donald G. - 202

Brody, Benjamin - 539
Brown, Daniel - 305
Brown, Terence - 356
Brustein, Robert - 221, 306, 500
Bryson, Rhett B. - 307
Buck, Richard M. - 503
Burns, Carolyn D. - 261
Byers, John A. - 438

Cahn, Judah - 212
Callahan, J. Stephen - 237
Calta, Louis - 142, 147, 213
Campbell, Mary E. - 262, 357
Canaday, Nicholas - 222
Carr, Duane R. - 459
Cavarozzi, Joyce P. - 196
Chapman, John - 263, 308
Chiari, J. - 214
Clurman, Harold - 126, 309, 382, 383, 488, 500, 504
Coale, Sam - 505
Coe, Richard M. - 506
Cohn, Ruby - 310, 311, 384, 385
Cook, Bruce - 264
Cooke, Richard P. - 265, 312
Corrigan, Robert W. - 460
Crinkley, Richmond - 313, 386
Crosland, Philip F. - 507

Crowther, Bosley - 223
Curry, Ryder H. - 266

Debusscher, Gilbert - 500
Delatte, Ann P. - 387
Dieb, Ronald K. - 314
Diehl, Digby - 128
Dillon, Perry C. - 268
Doerry, Karl W. - 441
Dollard, John - 461
Downer, Alan S. - 239
Dozier, Richard J. - 315
Duncan, Nancy K. - 316
Duplessis, Rachel B. - 448
Duprey, Richard A. - 240

Eichelbaum, Stanley - 180, 508
Ellis, Donald - 241
Ellison, Jerome - 215
Elsom, John - 462
Engle, William F. - 389
English, Emma Jean M. - 317
Esslin, Martin - 500, 568

Falb, Lewis - 463
Falk, Eugene, H. - 358
Finnigan, Jacqueline S. - 489
Fischer, Gretl K. - 318
Fitzgerald, J. - 242
Flatley, Guy - 128
Fleming, Wiliam P. - 443
Fletcher, William D. - 243
Fodor, Joan R. - 540
Forbes, Anthony - 269
Force, William M. - 319
Frankel, Haskel - 390
Franzblau, Abraham N. - 500
Freedman, Morris - 244
French, Paul D. - 245
Funke, Lewis - 162

Gabbard, Lucinda P. - 541
Gaines, Robert A. - 320
Gale, William - 542

Garza, Esmeralda - 490
Gassner, John - 270
Getlein, Frank - 543
Gill, Brendan - 271, 321, 391, 509, 544
Gilman, Richard - 392
Gilmore, S. - 578
Gortner, Richard - 367
Gottfried, Martin, 272, 273, 322, 393, 510, 545
Gross, Theodore - 167
Guernsey, Otis L. - 121, 323, 359, 394, 443, 463, 491, 511, 546, 569
Gussow, Mel - 445

Hall, Roger A. - 446
Halperen, Max - 274
Hamblen, Abigail A. - 275
Hankiss, Elmer - 204
Harris, Leonard - 276, 324, 395
Harte, Barbara - 163, 164
Hartnoll, Phyllis - 158
Hazard, Forrest E. - 277
Hefling, Joel - 360
Hempel, Peter - 547
Hewes, Henry - 325, 396, 500, 512
Higgins, David M. - 398
Higgins, John - 513
Hill, Linda M. - 514
Hinds, Carolyn M. - 399
Hobson, Harold - 246
Holtan, Orley I. - 465
Hopkins, Anthony - 466
Hopper, Stanley R. - 467
Houghton, Norris - 400
Hughes, Catherine - 401, 515, 548, 549
Hull, Elizabeth A. - 516
Hurley, Paul J. - 216

Irwin, Robert - 550

Jackson, Esther M. - 467
Jansky, Ann Leah L. - 326
Jefferys, Allan - 278
Johnson, Martha J. - 247
Johnson, Malcolm L. - 140, 518, 570, 571
Jones, Donna Mae - 205

Kahan, Gerald - 160, 169
Kalem, T.E. - 401, 519, 551
Kauffman, Stanley - 225, 327, 403, 520
Kelly, Edward - 226
Kerensky, Oleg - 279
Kerr, Walter - 227, 280, 281, 328, 329, 404
Kilkner, M.J. - 404
Kingsley, Lawrence - 469
Kitchin, Laurence - 228
Kissel, Howard - 521, 552
Kolin, Phillip C. - 330, 470
Kroll, Jack - 331, 405, 522, 553, 573

La Belle, Jenijoy - 554
Lambert, J.W. - 332, 361, 407, 447
Langdon, Harry N. - 362
Lask, Thomas - 116, 118
Laufe, Abe - 229
Lauricella, James - 206
Lazier, Gil - 492
Lee, Robert A. - 363
Lee, Robert C. - 282
Lenz, Harold - 471
Lester, Elenore - 123, 184
Levene, Victoria E. - 448
Levine, Mordecai H. - 248
Levy, Valerie B - 364
Lewis, Allan - 365
Lewis, Theophilus - 333
Leyden, William H. - 408
Loeffler, Donald L. - 523
Long, Mary - 137

Loynd, Ray - 524
Lucey, William F. - 334
Lumley, Frederick - 449

Mah, Kai-Ho - 574
Mandanis, Alice - 335
Marshall, Thomas F. - 283
Matlaw, Myron - 171
Matthews, Honor - 249
McCants, Sarah M. - 493
McMurrian, Jaqueline Y. - 230
Melloan, George - 409
Meyer, Ruth - 284
Miller, Joanne - 525
Moore, Don D. - 450
Moritz, Charles - 151
Morsberger, Robert E. - 472
Morse, Ben - 207
Mullin, Donald - 556
Murray, Michael - 410
Mussoff, L. - 336
Myers, Charles R. - 401
Myers, Joseph T. - 412

Neblett, Joseph M. - 495
Nelson, Benjamin - 285
Nemy, Enid - 170
Newman, Edwin - 413
Nilan, Mary M. - 473
Norton, Rictor C. - 414
Novick, Julius - 415

Oakes, Philip - 138
O'Connor, John - 557
Olin, Carol - 250
Otten Terry - 286
Page, Michael - 575
Palazzo, Laura - 251
Paolucci, Anne - 451, 474, 500
Parsarathy, R. - 252
Paul, Louis - 253
Pearre, Howard - 231

Pease, Donald - 416
Popkin, Henry - 165
Porte, Michael - 266
Porter, Thomas E. - 337
Post, Robert M. - 338, 339
Probst, Leonard - 287, 340, 527

Quigley, Martin - 368
Quinn, James P. - 496

Ramsey, Roger - 417
Rand, Calvin - 341
Richardson, James G. - 418
Richmond, Hugh M. - 419
Rigdon, Walter - 155
Riley, Carolyn - 163, 164
Rissover, Frederic - 420
Rogoff, Gordon - 576
Roth, Emilou - 342
Roth, Philip - 500
Ruben, Paul A. - 368
Rudin, Seymour - 421
Rudisell, Cecil W. - 422
Rule, Margaret - 458
Rutenberg, Michael E. - 120, 124, 217, 288, 343, 500

Sanders, Kevin - 527, 558
Sanders, Walter E. - 344
Sandoe, James - 289, 345
Sapoznik, Ran - 529
Sayre, Nora - 475
Schechner, Richard - 500
Schneider, Alan - 500
Schneider, Howard - 131
Schneider, Ruth M. - 476
Shubeck, John - 423
Schwartz, Jerry - 142
Sellin, Eric - 346
Sheed, Wilfred - 424
Shelton, Lewis - 370
Shorey, Kenneth P. - 559
Shorter, Eric - 347, 560

Shupbach, Deanna J. - 369
Shuster, Alvin - 371
Simon, John - 290, 531
Simpson, Herbert M. - 291
Skloot, Robert - 292
Smith, Bruce M. - 497
Smith, Rebecca L. - 532
Solomon, Jerry - 208
Stace, Ann C. - 209
Stambusky, Alan A. - 152, 156
Stark, John - 452
Stavrou, C.N. - 532
Steadman, Dan - 348
Steiner, Donald L. - 453
Stephens, Suzanne S. - 454
Stern, Daniel - 139
Stewart, R.S. - 500
Storrer, William A. - 293
Styan, J.L. - 294
Sullivan, Dan - 232, 295, 296
Sykes, Carol A. - 477
Syna, Sy - 425
Sysa, Glenna - 135

Tanner, Henry - 148
Taylor, Charlene M. - 478
Taylor, Robert - 533
Terrien, Samuel - 219, 372
Thompson, Howard - 233, 455
Tolpegin, Dorothy D. - 426
Toohey, John L. - 159
Trilling, Diana - 500
Tucker, John B. - 351
Tynan, Kenneth - 254

Ulanov, Barry - 210
Umberger, Norman C. - 375

Von Ransom, Brooks - 141
Von Szeliski, John - 374
Vos, Nelvin - 297, 479

Wagner, Marlene S. - 427
Wallace, Robert S. - 480

Wardle, Irving - 125, 352, 376, 456
Watt, Douglas - 428, 535, 561, 577
Watts, Richard - 298, 353, 429, 562
Way, Brian - 255, 500
Weales, Gerald - 299, 354, 500
Weiler, A.H. - 166, 168
Weilwarth, George - 430
West, Anthony - 300
Westerfield, William - 431
White, James E. - 377, 481
Whitman, Alden - 172
Wilderman, Marie R. - 432
Willeford, William - 355
Willis, N.J. - 579

Wilson, Edwin - 536, 563
Wilson, Garff B. - 482
Wilson, Raymond J. - 483
Wimble, Barton - 433
Winehall, Cedric R. - 434
Wines, Mildred H. - 211
Witherington, Paul - 378
Woods, Linda - 301
Wurster, G.S. - 564

Yerby, Loree - 117

Zahn, Douglas - 492
Zimbardo, Rose - 500
Zindel, Paul - 117
Zolotow, Sam - 150, 157

Appendix B

PLAY TITLES INDEX

All Over
Editions and Anthologies - 34, 35, 36, 77
Interviews - 129, 136
Biography - 170, 174
Criticism - 433, 440, 451, 471, 479, 500, 526, 555
Dissertations - 447, 485, 494, 502, 516, 540, 547
Play Reviews:
    New York, 27 March 1971, Martin Beck Theater, Director John Gielgud - 380, 382, 383, 386, 390, 391, 393, 395, 397, 401, 402, 403, 404, 406, 409, 410, 413, 415, 421, 423, 428, 429, 473, 488, 548
    London, 31 Jan. 1972, Aldwych Theater, Director Peter Hall, Royal Shakespeare Co. - 447, 456
    Hartford, Nov. 1975, Hartford Stage Company - 518
    Brighton (Eng.), Winter 1976, Garden Centre, Director Patrick Lau - 560
Television Reviews:
    PBS Theater in America presentation, April 1976 - 543, 557

The American Dream
Manuscripts and Special Collections - 25, 26
Editions and Anthologies - 37, 38, 78, 79
Interviews - 116, 120
Biography - 143, 169, 172, 183
Criticism - 216, 222, 235, 240, 244, 255, 273, 274, 283, 294, 297, 304, 305, 311, 330, 338, 343, 363, 377, 378, 399, 400, 405, 420, 430, 442, 449, 450, 451, 458, 463, 469, 470, 479, 500, 522, 530
Dissertations - 268, 369, 370, 381, 408, 434, 448, 485, 493, 494, 502, 514, 516, 540, 547

Theses - 387, 389, 432
Play Reviews:
>New York, 24 Jan. 1961, York Playhouse - 270, 473, 488, 548
>London, 24 Oct. 1961, Royal Court Theatre, director Peter Yates - 193
>New York, 2 Oct. 1968, Billy Rose Theater, director Edward Albee, Playwrights Repertory Theater - 296

The Ballad of the Sad Cafe
Manuscripts and Special Collections - 6, 17, 18
Editions and Anthologies - 39, 40
Interviews - 117, 118, 120, 124
Criticism - 203, 240, 273, 304, 305, 329, 330, 343, 458, 470, 500, 523
Dissertations - 485, 494, 516
Theses - 307, 388, 418, 490
Play Reviews:
>New York, 30 Oct. 1963, Martin Beck Theater, Director Alan Schneider - 197, 207, 210, 270
>Worcester, Eng., Autumn 1969, Director John Hope-Mason, Worcester Repertory Company - 347
>London, March 1971, Thorndike Theatre, Director Leonard White - 379, 407

Bartleby
Dissertations - 434
Play Reviews:
>New York, 24 Jan. 1961, York Playhouse - 193

Box and *Quotations from Chairman Mao Tse-Tung*
Manuscripts and Special Collections - 33
Editions and Anthologies - 41, 42, 43, 44, 80, 81, 87
Interviews - 124
Biography - 174
Criticism - 302, 310, 330, 343, 345, 365, 373, 384, 385, 400, 405, 430, 451, 458, 466, 470, 500, 530, 556
Dissertations - 317, 408, 494, 502, 516, 547
Theses - 387
Play Reviews:
>Buffalo, 7 March 1968, Buffalo Studio Arena Theater, Director Alan Schneider - 257, 280
>Spoleto, Italy, July 1968, Director Alan Schneider - 279
>New York, 30 Sept. 1968, Billy Rose Theater, Director Alan Schneider - 263, 264, 265, 267, 271, 272, 276, 278, 281, 287, 290, 298, 299, 300, 341

Breakfast at Tiffany's
Biography - 157
Play Reviews:
    New York, Dec. 1966 - 232

Counting the Ways and *Listening*
Editions and Anthologies - 45
Interviews - 138, 140, 141
Criticism - 567, 575
Play Reviews:
    (*CW* only) London, Dec. 1976, National Theatre - 568
    (*CW* and *L*) Hartford, 28 Jan. 1977, Director Edward Albee, Hartford Stage Company - 565, 570, 571, 573, 576, 577

The Death of Bessie Smith
Manuscripts and Special Collections - 25
Editions and Anthologies - 82
Interviews - 117, 120
Biography - 143
Criticism - 194, 216, 228, 240, 274, 283, 304, 305, 311, 330, 338, 343, 363, 405, 448, 449, 451, 458, 468, 470, 473, 500, 530
Dissertations - 369, 408, 434, 493, 494, 502, 516, 547
Play Reviews:
    New York, 1 March 1961, York Playhouse - 270, 488
    ondon, 24 Oct. 1961, Royal Court Theatre, Director Peter Yates - 193
    New York, 2 Oct. 1968, Billy Rose Theater, Director Michael Kahn, Playwrights Repertory Theater - 296
Television Reviews:
    London, Granada Television Production, June 1965 - 218

A Delicate Balance
Editions and Anthologies - 45, 83
Interviews - 121, 124
Biography - 159, 174
Criticism - 231, 233, 235, 239, 242, 259, 273, 288, 294, 297, 304, 305, 311, 330, 338, 339, 343, 354, 356, 363, 365, 371, 374, 378, 400, 405, 430, 437, 442, 448, 451, 458, 462, 463, 469, 470, 478, 487, 500, 526
Dissertations - 268, 370, 382, 408, 441, 485, 494, 502, 516, 540, 547
Theses - 316, 387, 422, 436, 446, 479, 484
Play Reviews:
    New York, 22 Sept. 1966, Martin Beck Theater, Director Alan Schneider - 227, 238, 270, 424, 548
    Paris, Nov. 1967, Odéon Theater, Director Jean-Louis Barrault - 234, 246

Film Reviews:
>1973, American Film Artists Series - 476, 559

Everything in the Garden
Editions and Anthologies - 47, 48, 49
Interviews - 124
Criticism - 256, 269, 289, 330, 338, 343, 365, 385, 458, 470, 479, 482, 500
Dissertations - 407, 494, 516
Theses - 430
Play Reviews:
>New York, 29 Nov. 1967, Plymouth Theater, Director Peter Glenville - 306, 329

Fam and Yam
Criticism - 343
Dissertations - 317, 434, 494, 502

Malcolm
Manuscripts and Special Collections - 31
Editions and Anthologies - 50, 84
Interviews - 121, 124
Criticism - 235, 273, 304, 305, 329, 330, 458, 470, 500, 523
Dissertations - 408, 485, 494, 516
Play Reviews:
>New York, 11 Jan. 1966, Shubert Theater, Director Alan Schneider - 306

The Sandbox
Editions and Anthologies - 51, 52, 53, 54, 55, 56, 85
Interviews - 120
Biography - 169
Criticism - 194, 240, 244, 273, 294, 297, 304, 305, 311, 330, 338, 343, 377, 400, 405, 451, 458, 468, 470, 479, 500, 530
Dissertations - 268, 369, 408, 434, 485, 493, 494, 502, 516, 547
Theses - 387

Schism
Editions and Anthologies - 57
Criticism - 377

Seascape
Editions and Anthologies - 58, 59, 86
Interviews - 131, 133
Criticism - 501, 503
Dissertations - 502, 547
Play Reviews:
    Philadelphia, Jan. 1975, Forrest Theater, Director Edward Albee - 507, 517
    New York, 26 Jan. 1975, Shubert Theater, Director Edward Albee - 498, 499, 504, 505, 509, 510, 512, 513, 515, 519, 520, 521, 522, 527, 528, 531, 535, 536, 548
    Los Angeles, April 1975, Director Edward Albee - 524, 534

Tiny Alice
Editions and Anthologies - 60, 61, 62, 87
Interviews - 120, 121, 123, 124
Biography - 153, 162, 174, 176, 177, 178, 179, 180
Criticism - 212, 219, 224, 235, 240, 262, 266, 273, 283, 291, 292, 297, 304, 305, 310, 311, 329, 330, 334, 335, 338, 343, 350, 354, 355, 357, 363, 365, 377, 378, 400, 405, 416, 426, 430, 439, 448, 449, 452, 458, 467, 469, 470, 473, 479, 481, 482, 500, 506, 523, 525, 530
Dissertations - 268, 314, 362, 369, 370, 382, 408, 441, 453, 485, 493, 494, 502, 547
Play Reviews:
    New York, Dec. 1964, Billy Rose Theater, Director Alan Schneider - 270, 329, 488, 548
    New York, 29 Sept. 1969, ANTA Theater, Director William Ball, American Conservatory Theater - 303, 308, 309, 312, 313, 321, 322, 324, 325, 327, 328, 331, 333, 340, 349, 351, 353, 392
    London, 15 Jan. 1970, Aldwych Theater, Director Robin Phillips, Royal Shakespeare Company - 361, 366, 376
    Hartford, 31 March 1972, Director Paul Weidner, Hartford Stage Company - 445
    San Francisco, 4 Oct. 1975, Geary Theater, Director William Ball, American Conservatory Theater - 508, 533

Who's Afraid of Virginia Woolf?
Manuscripts and Special Collections - 19, 27, 29, 33
Editions and Anthologies - 64, 65, 66, 67, 68, 88, 89
Biography - 144, 146, 149, 150, 169, 174

150 EDWARD ALBEE

Criticism - 195, 199, 200, 204, 214, 216, 228, 229, 235, 240, 244, 247, 253, 268, 273, 274, 275, 277, 283, 284, 286, 294, 297, 304, 305, 310, 311, 315, 318, 329, 330, 337, 338, 343, 354, 358, 363, 367, 372, 378, 400, 405, 414, 419, 425, 435, 438, 442, 448, 449, 451, 457, 458, 459, 460, 461, 462, 463, 465, 469, 470, 472
Dissertations - 268, 293, 314, 317, 344, 369, 370, 381, 414, 441, 453, 483, 485, 493, 494, 502, 516, 540, 547
Play Reviews:
    New York, 13 Oct. 1962, Billy Rose Theater, Director Alan Schneider - 254, 270, 392, 473, 488
    London, 6 Feb. 1964, Piccadilly Theater, Director Alan Schneider - 201
    New York, 3 July 1968, Forum Theater, Director Mira Trailovie, Ateljie 212 - 295
    New York, 13 Oct. 1972, Gramercy Arts Theater, Director Rene Buch, Spanish Theater Repertory Company - 455
    Boston, Feb. 1976, Colonial Theater, Director Edward Albee - 542
    New York, 1 April 1976, Music Box Theater, Director Edward Albee - 537, 538, 539, 544, 545, 549, 551, 552, 553, 558, 561, 562, 563
Film Reviews:
    Warner Brothers, 1966, Director Mike Nichols - 223, 225

The Zoo Story
Manuscripts and Special Collections - 26
Editions and Anthologies - 69, 70, 71, 72, 73, 74, 75, 76, 90
Interviews - 116, 117, 120
Biography - 169, 183
Criticism - 194, 228, 235, 240, 244, 248, 249, 255, 273, 274, 297, 301, 304, 305, 310, 311, 319, 329, 330, 336, 338, 343, 344, 354, 363, 400, 405, 417, 430, 449, 451, 458, 463, 468, 469, 470, 473, 477, 480, 492, 523, 526, 530, 541, 550, 566
Dissertations - 268, 314, 369, 381, 407, 411, 433, 441, 447, 452, 476, 493, 494, 502, 516, 547
Theses - 205, 387, 389, 421, 489, 499
Play Reviews:
    New York, 14 Jan. 1960, Provincetown Playhouse - 473, 488, 548
    New York, 8 June 1965, Cherry Lane Theater, Director Alan Schneider, Playwrights Repertory - 213
    New York, 9 Oct. 1968, Billy Rose Theater, Director Richard Barr, Playwrights Repertory - 258